VIEWS FROM THE HILL

THE STORY OF WHITLEY

and

Memories of Whitley Life in Times Past

By

Dennis Wood CEng MIET

Best wishes

Dennis

28 october 2017

ISBN 978-0-9935512-4-6

Front cover: "Cows at Whitley Park Farm". Oil on canvas painting unsigned and undated but thought to be c. 1860. Acquired from Lowerwood Farm, Shinfield. Reproduced by kind permission of the Museum of English Rural Life, University of Reading, ref: 64/56.

Dedication page: Christ Church, looking at the east window from Christchurch Road and also the old vicarage to the left, 1880s.

Back Cover: The east window of Christ Church looking from the nave of the church.

Published by Scallop Shell Press

29 Derby Road,

Caversham,

Reading.

RG4 5HE

DEDICATION

This book is dedicated to the memory of my greatly loved and missed son, Paul, who passed away far too soon at the age of 19 years in 1987.

This book is also dedicated to my late parents-in-law, Joan and Stan, who both spent nearly all their lives in Whitley.

ACKNOWLEDGEMENTS

It is with grateful thanks that I acknowledge the help, advice, time and encouragement given by the following people:

David Cliffe (formerly of the Local Studies Library) and Katie Amos and their colleagues at the Reading Central Library for extensive assistance with locating information from directories, electoral rolls, censuses, and the many books. Also for allowing me to use the old photographic images on the dedication page and on pages 29, 31, 37, 40, 41, 47, 50, 51, 53, 56, 57, 60, 61, 62, 74, 90, 91, 94, 95, 112, 117, 125, 132, 133, 134

Caroline Gould (Museum of English Rural Life) at the University of Reading for assisting in locating historical information and the image of old Whitley Park Farm.

Andrew Palmer and Howard Palmer QC for their help with the Palmer family and the Cobham family.

Sue Brock and Hilary Munro who gave helpful information about the Sutton family.

Sue Bourne (Head of The Avenue School) who allowed me to research the old school log books and to use the collected information and the photographs of the Open-Air School in Chapter 9.

Jane Burrell-Wood (Abbey School Old Girls Association) who was very helpful with advice on the history of the Abbey School.

Ian Boyd who helped with information on the Goodrest Estate and Crosfields School.

Sidney Gold for advice on the architects of Reading.

John Winters for his information on Smallmead Stadium.

Joan van Emden for her constructive help and advice on the format of the book.

John G Mullaney at Scallop Shell Press for all his help with publication of the book.
John R Mullaney for production of the cover and the bespoke maps.

All the contributors to the Memories part – Peggy, Patrick, Barbara, Melvyn, Patricia and Pearl – and for the helpful information that they have provided as well about Whitley area.

And especially my wife, Pearl, for her support and help to get the book completed!

CONTENTS

Introduction

Whitley has a rich and varied history and has been a land of huge contrasts during its existence. The main contrast has been between the parts which covered the top of the surrounding hill (Christchurch Road and Shinfield Road through to the top of Whitley Wood) and the lower Whitley level which ran down to the River Kennet and the Foudry Brook. In early days of settlement, the hill top was the wooded area while the lower level led down to marshes and flood plains. With the gradual need for a road to Shinfield along the hill top, the wooded area was opened up and the surrounding land was developed as park land for the gentry in the 18th and 19th centuries. The road to Basingstoke and Southampton was opened up along the lower level, but above the flood plains, and acted as an enclosing barrier to this area which was later developed as farm land, particularly by the monks of Reading Abbey. Both these developments started from the Saxon period onwards.

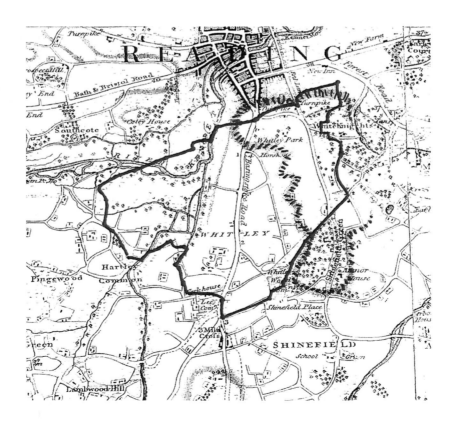

The first map, on the previous page, shows the old boundary of the Manor of Whitley superimposed on a map drawn by Thomas Pride, c 1790. It also shows the routes through Whitley of the road to Basingstoke and the road to Shinfield (then known as Shinefield) together with the road near the northern boundary that joins the two, then called Southern Hill. The main hill slopes which so much defined the contrasting parts of Whitley are highlighted. The flow of the river Kennet and the adjoining Foudry Brook can also be seen on the west side of Whitley Manor.

Even when the major Victorian development of what is now Christchurch Road and Upper Redlands Road started, the contrast continued. The Central Whitley lower level to the east of the Basingstoke Road continued to be farm land until the end of the 19th century and only started to change through the first half of the 20th century. The higher level was developed for the wealthier business residents of the town while the farm land was gradually replaced with housing estates. Eventually, after the Second World War, the houses of the higher level were either demolished and replaced with more modern properties or converted into school buildings, hotels, etc. The wealthier residents had started to move away around the time of the First World War into country estates, consequent on the much easier transport of the time and the improved road surfaces.

Meanwhile, from the 19th century, the western part of Whitley around the flood plains was starting to be used and this led to major development in the late 20th century as pressure grew to find new land for sporting and commercial properties and then for additional residential areas around the growing town of Reading.

However, let us step back a couple of hundred years before all this major development took place.

It is interesting to read the impressions of previous generations when considering how a particular place or area appeared to people who lived and travelled the area in past centuries. In this chapter some 18th and 19th century descriptions are used to illustrate how authors of the time viewed Whitley and its immediate surroundings.

The following first description is from J Robertson's compilation from the mid-19th century and gives a useful picture of how Whitley and its surrounding areas appeared, as the traveller left Reading town, and some of its ownership through that period:

We will pause for a while on the summit of the eminence in which Southampton St. terminates to gaze on the two pictures of Reading behind us, and then proceed to the turn-pike, where opens as fine a picture as the eye would wish to dwell upon. A large portion of Hampshire lies 'smiling before us', bounded on the right by hills that crown the valley of the Kennet – on the left by the thickly wooded district of Whiteknights and Maiden Erleigh. Here commences the Hamlet of Whitley, (forming part of St Giles' parish), once an appendage to the Abbey of Reading. Queen Mary granted the manor to Sir Francis Englefield from whom it passed to the Vachells. When the estates of that family were purchased by Col. Thompson, Whitley Manor was included in the sale. It is now the property of Miss Frances Jennings. Whitley Park, called by Leland 'the Abbot's Park at the entrance of Reading', is now a park in name only – the greater part of it being in a state of cultivation. It was granted by Queen Elizabeth to Sir Francis Knollys, and was at a later period the seat of the Kendricks. Its present owners are Messrs Allotson and Bros of London.

After clearing the Whitley Gate, and passing several villas in the course of erection on the right, the road continues to descend for a considerable distance. The lands on either side are highly cultivated and the views extremely beautiful – particularly one on the right, of Coley House and the Valley of the Kennet, and, on the left, of Goodrest Lodge and Park, occupying the side of the hill. A little farther on the left stands Whitley Lodge, the residence of T. Owst, esq.
[From "The Environs of Reading Vol. 1", edited by J. Robertson, 1843].

The following description is from Mary Russell Mitford's book, 'Belford Regis', and gives a very idyllic rural picture of Whitley in the mid-19th century but she travels from the other direction:

The approach to [Reading from Three Mile Cross], straight as a dart, runs along a wide and populous turn-pike road…, all alive with carts and coaches, wagons and phaetons, horse people and foot people; and the borders…. become more thickly inhabited as we draw nearer to the metropolis of the county: to say nothing of the three cottages all in a row, with two small houses detached, which a board affixed to one of them informs the passer-by is 'Two-Mile Cross';……or the series of buildings called the Long [Barn], terminating at the end next the road with an old-fashioned and most picturesque public house, with pointed roofs, and benches at the door, and round the large elm before it.

No sooner do we get to within a mile of the town, than our approach is indicated by successive market-gardens on either side, crowned as we ascend the long hill on which the turnpike-gate stands, by an extensive nursery-ground….. Then the turnpike-gate, with its civil keeper – then another public-house – then the clear bright pond on the top of the hill....

About this point, where one road ....diverges from the great southern entrance, and where two streets meeting or parting lead by separate ways down the steep hill to the centre of the town, stands a handsome mansion, surrounded by orchards and pleasure-grounds; across which is...to be seen the very best view of [Reading], with its long range of modern buildings in the outskirts, mingled with picturesque old street; the venerable old towers of [St Mary's and St Laurence's]; the light and tapering spire of [St Giles'];......

Nobody can look at [Reading] from this point, without feeling that it is a very charming scene.
[From 'Belford Regis' by Mary Russell Mitford, 1835]

These descriptions both refer to the two views looking down into the town, one down Southampton Street (to St Mary's and St Giles') and the other down Silver Street (to St Laurence's and the Abbey ruins). They also refer to the view looking away from the town to the open farm land of Central Whitley surrounded by the hill ridges to the north, east and south, with buildings starting to appear on the road to Shinfield and the road to Basingstoke. Mitford's book extract also refers to the Four Horseshoes Inn, the Long Barn cottages next door, the Whitley turnpike on the hill, the King's Head public house on the Reading-Whitley boundary at the top of the hill and the King's Head Pond on the corner of the two roads. The 'handsome mansion' to which she refers was Highgrove House, at the top of Silver St. The panorama remained largely like that until the end of the 19th century by which time more extensive development was about to get under way.

In his 'History of Reading' published in 1835, John Doran's record of the Beating of the Bounds of Reading in 1714 was detailed and it explained that the Hamlet and Manor of Whitley extended westwards for some distance beyond the river Kennet before meeting the parish of Burghfield. It is unclear whether this area of marshland (the river flood plain in the main) was included in the parish of St Giles in medieval times. Other than use of the river Kennet for water treatment works from the 19th century, the marshland to the west of it was not of any major significance to Whitley or Reading until the late 20th century when it was considered for development after land reclamation from the flood plains of the Kennet. However it is interesting to note the fact that Cut-throat Lane (clearly not a pleasant place to walk along!), which had been known previously as Perrin's Lane, was described as extending right down to the meadow alongside the river Kennet at that time. This lane was shortened once the brick-making companies along Katesgrove Lane, especially the Waterloo Kiln, cut away the west side of the hill to extract the clay. As a result, Milman Road, as the lane became, stops abruptly at the edge of the steep drop down to the Robert Cort industrial estate that now exists at the lower level below.

The historic boundary of the Manor, just before being taken into Reading Borough in 1887, ran roughly north-east from the river Kennet (close to Waterloo Meadows) through Milman Road to Basingstoke Road at Christchurch Gardens, then north to the Whitley Street roundabout then east along Christchurch Road through to Upper Redlands Road. From Eastern Avenue it passed almost directly south through Whiteknights Park, most of Leighton Park to Elm Lane, then south-west through Whitley Wood to the M4 at Whitley Wood Lane junction, west by the M4 Junction 11 to include Worton Grange, the Madejski Stadium and Green Park. Finally, it passed north around Fobney Meadow to re-join the Kennet at the south of Waterloo Meadow. This boundary very much followed the ridge along from Whitley Street to Whiteknights, then the ridge south to Shinfield Green and then the ridge west through Whitley Wood until it ends; from there it enclosed the Foudry Brook and followed the river Kennet and passed back up the ridge to Whitley Street to form the lower level which leads down to the flood plains of the river and brook. The top of the ridge is formed from what is known as London Clay, covered in part with a layer of Boyn Hill gravel, and the bottom of the lower level is clay, running down to the waterways, with sand layers in the middle levels of the ridge.

The book is in two parts. The first part focusses on the detailed history and development of the entirety of Whitley. The second part gives a selection of memories of Whitley life over the last ninety years or so.

PART 1

The Story of Whitley

Chapter 1

Early History and the creation of the Manor of Whitley

The area that became known as Whitley was used by early travellers during the prehistoric period, particularly the hill tops surrounding its lower level. During the Old Stone Age, more than 150,000 years ago, flint material from the gravel on Southern Hill (the hill-top along the ridge from Katesgrove to Whiteknights) was used for making hand axes and scrapers. Samples have been discovered around Christ Church and along Shinfield Road. In the Middle Stone Age, after the last Ice Age, which ended 12,000 years ago, the Kennet side was much used by the hunter-gatherers and flint artefacts have been found near the old Sewage Works and also near Bourne Avenue in this area. Much of the wooded land was being cleared and settlement started during the New Stone Age, less than 4000 years ago. Flint axes from this period have been unearthed in Christchurch Gardens, Pepper Lane and near Christ Church, while a flint arrowhead was found in Northcourt Avenue near Wellington Avenue.

There was much more settlement during the Iron and Bronze Ages. What is thought to be a Bronze Age barrow with a partial ring ditch was discovered at the old Sewage Works at Manor Farm. A disc barrow containing an urn was found on Marshall's Hill (Cressingham Road) in 1907. A bronze spearhead was also unearthed on Marshall's Hill. Iron Age coins have been found in the area of the Engineer's Arms in Whitley Wood and also in Milman Road. In 1905, an earthenware Iron Age cup was discovered in the area near the Newcastle Road allotments in an old gravel pit.

Once settlements had been established and trading between communities began, fortifications using hill forts were introduced. The routes from Basingstoke and Shinfield into Reading became well-used thoroughfares for travellers. Evidence of an old Iron Age field system was revealed at Little Lea Farm on the outskirts of Whitley. Reading itself continued to be mainly a transient settling place rather than a permanent settlement until after the Romans started to develop the area with Calleva Atrebatum forming their local community at Silchester. Roman pottery, coins and other pieces have been found at Manor Farm and at the site of the old Rose Kiln. Excavations along the Kennet flood plain area have revealed that land west of Basingstoke Road was an area of settlement during the Bronze Age and Roman times with ditches, enclosures and gullies in place. A Roman stone quern has been unearthed in Northcourt Avenue and other Roman coins found in Brixham Road, in

Greenfields Road and at the top of Cressingham Road. A coffin from the Saxon period was found at Smallmead.

Gradually the area of Whitley was developed as open farm land during the Romano-British period, then the Saxon period under Danish rule and through to the Norman invasion in the 11th century by which time it was established as the 'Manor of Whitley' in its own right.

The Domesday Book of 1086 describes the Manor of Whitley in the Reading *hundred* and this is covered in the next chapter. Also identified were some other manors adjacent to Whitley as being in existence at that time: Hartley and Burghfield (in the Reading *hundred*, alongside Whitley and Reading town), together with Shinfield (in the adjacent Charlton *hundred*). A *hundred* was a Saxon description of a district which had a large village surrounded by a number of smaller settlements, farms and fields.

Hartley

The Manor of Hartley is described in the Domesday Book as follows: *Ragenhild held it from King Edward. Then it answered for 2 hides; now for 1 hide. Land for 2 ploughs. Nothing in lordship but 2 villagers and 3 smallholders have 2 ploughs. Woodland at 15 pigs. Value 40s.*

The small Manor of Hartley is no longer separate but forms part of the parish of Shinfield. It is not shown on today's maps but was located to the west of the Basingstoke Road away from Whitley Wood common land sitting between Whitley, Three Mile Cross and Burghfield. However there is still Hartley Court Farm, off Hartley Court Road, just south of the M4 as a reminder of its existence. The manor house of Hartley Court was built early in the 16th Century for the Beke family and, with an 18th century frontage added, still exists adjacent to the farm today as a listed building. It was mentioned in J. Robertson's book 'The Environs of Reading' in 1843, as follows, referring to the Shinfield parish church of St Mary's:

It contains... a mural monument, representing a knight in armour, and opposite him a lady, veiled, with a younger female figure. From the Latin inscription below, we learn it is in memory of H. Beke esq, of Hartley Court, his wife Jane, and his daughter Eliza – the date is obliterated.

Henry Beke lived in the early 16th century and was from the Beke family that also owned the Whiteknights estate at that time, but apparently he preferred to live at Hartley Court. In 1606, Sir Francis Englefield acquired the estate which passed to Sir Thomas Smyth in 1609 and was then sold on to various others including William Wilder.

J. Robertson then says:

In the year 1709, the manor of Hartley was conveyed by its then possessor, John Westmoreland, esq, to Sir Owen Buckingham, knt, by the description of the manor and liberty of Hartley Battle (its original title) with all its rights and appurtenances, being parcel of the manor of Brightwalton or Brickelton in the county of Berks. The whole...... came into the possession of H Plant esq, whose devisees sold them...... to William Dearsly esq. At his decease they were inherited by his son, William H Dearsly esq. He died in 1825 and his widow married Thomas Owst esq of Keyingham in Holderness, Yorkshire, who became lord of the manor in right of his wife.

It is recorded that the Benyon family at Englefield, who then owned Hartley Court, rented out the property at the turn of the 20th century to Edward VII and his mistress, Lillie Langtry, used it in her later life.

Shinfield

Bordering the south and east of Whitley was the Manor of Shinfield. This Manor was listed in the Domesday Book as being in the Hundred of Charlton. Its area covered the present villages of Swallowfield, Spencer's Wood and Three Mile Cross as well as Shinfield itself and reached south as far as the Loddon River. It may also have extended into the southern part of present Whitley at one time as manorial estate owners bought and sold land. Much of this land originally belonged to Reading Abbey and later passed to the Crown after the Dissolution of the Monasteries.

The old Shinfield manor house used to be along Shinfield Green on the opposite side to the present-day European Centre for Medium-Range Weather Forecasts, just north of the double-roundabout and the M4. It existed at the time of Henry VIII and became his property. From then it was held by various lords of the manor and was eventually demolished by Alexander Cobham in 1802. In 1923, it was described as having stood in a *'little paddock adjoining old barn and buildings called Ducketts, now owned by Reading University'*. This referred to Duckett's Farm, which became part of the University's Shinfield Farm land.

Burghfield

Abutting the west of Whitley and Hartley was the Manor of Burghfield (Borgefelle), listed in the Domesday Book as being in the Hundred of Reading. Burghfield had two Manors – Burghfield Regis and Burghfield Abbas - and was later extended to include Soefeld (Sheffield) Manor as part of the parish of Burghfield. The north of the parish is mainly dedicated to the upstream part of the river Kennet and the M4 between Junction 11 and Junction 12. The land adjacent to Whitley is largely flood plain, gravel pits/lakes and farm land and therefore has had no real impact on the development of Whitley.

Chapter 2

History of the Hamlet and Manor of Whitley and of Whitley Park

The Manor of Whitley had been open farm land from the earliest times and, during the Middle Ages, was under the stewardship of the monks at Reading Abbey. Most of it was attached to part of the Manor of Reading to form the parish of St Giles (the remainder being in the parish of Shinfield). In his document of 1960 on the 'Whitley Deeds of the Twelfth Century', C. F. Slade refers to several deeds which contain information on the creation of a park in the Whitley Manor not long after the Reading Abbey had been built. It appears that the Abbey obtained land in the north-east of the manor, in the area of what became Whitley Park Farm and adjacent to the Manor of Earley. This was permitted by King Henry II for use to create a park, for which 53 acres were allocated through a deal with the former owner and over time this was gradually increased to 100 acres or more. The Abbey continued to obtain more land in the manor during the 13th century and allowed Peter de Cosham to use the land on a lease basis.

Whitley Park was a haven for the monks with pleasure grounds and fishponds. From the Middle Ages, this was bounded by the Manor of Reading to the north, the Manor of Earley Whiteknights to the east, the Manor of Shinfield to the east and south and the Manor of Hartley to the west.

Although at the time it was not part of the domain of the church of St Giles, Whitley had already been identified in the Domesday Book in 1086 in its own right within the *Hundred* of Reading and within the Shire of Berkshire, its landowners being subject to the tax known as Danegeld. The Domesday Survey lists the manor of Witelei (as it was then described) as being assessed at 1 *hide*, having previously been at 3 hides. *There is land for 3 ploughs. On the demesne is 1 plough and 2 villeins and 2 bordars with 1 plough. There are 4 serfs and 12 acres of meadow and a fishing worth 40 pence, it is and was worth 40 shillings.* Thus the area was much smaller than it became later but notably it did reach the river Kennet to provide fishing access - this must have been just south of the community at Katesgrove. A *villein* was a peasant responsible to the Lord of the manor for paying rent and any taxes called for and he held a strip of land with certain rights and privileges. The *bordar* was a peasant with less land who provided labour to the villein or Lord.

Charles Coates, in his 'History and Antiquities of Reading' (1802), records that *before the reign of Henry II, Peter de Cosham sold to the abbey all his lands in Whitley, within and without the borough of Reading, for which he received 80 pounds and an annual present of a bezant of gold, in value about nine shillings. This was reduced by Thurstan de Cosham to a pepper-corn rent. The original grant was registered in court, before the Justices itinerant; as appears in the charter of Henry II. In 1349, the abbey purchased 21 acres of land here, belonging to John de Sulkdene or Suthdene; and, in 1399, Gilbert de Hegfield gave a piece of land called 'La Lynch' near Cadelgrove, in the village of Whitley; and in the ninth, tenth and sixteenth years of Edward III licence was granted to William de Whitley to alienate 20 acres of land to the abbey of Reading.* So there was a gradual process of acquisition by Reading Abbey of the lands that formed the village, or hamlet, and manor of Whitley and, in fact, there has been strong evidence that the abbey had a building, used as a retreat with pleasure grounds and a large grange barn in what was called Whitley Park and this barn and an old inn 'The Three Horseshoes' (later to change to The Four Horseshoes) were near the junction of Basingstoke Road with Long Barn Lane (hence the origin of its name). Gradually then, the hamlet of Whitley became linked to Reading during the Middle Ages through its expanding population.

Shortly after King Henry VIII's dissolution of the Abbey in 1539, John Leland in his record of his travels described his approach to Reading through Whitley Park, *There is a park cumming into Reading town, longging to the late monastery there.*

According to John Man in his 'History and Antiquities of Reading' (1816), *The manors of Reading and Whitley appear to have been united in the time of the abbots and, as such, were given in the second year of king Edward VI to his uncle, the lord protector, on whose death soon after, they reverted to the crown, and were separated in the following reign, when queen Mary gave the manor of Whitley to sir Francis Englefield.*

However, it was not until the reign of Queen Elizabeth that the ownership of Whitley and its relationship with the borough of Reading stabilised after these four hundred years of change. Charles Coates further records of Whitley that *Queen Elizabeth, by her charter, gave 50 oaks, out of the park, to the corporation of Reading; and she granted the park itself, with all its rights, members, appurtenances, all houses and buildings, and all bucks and does, to sir Francis Knollys, knight, and dame Catherine, his wife.* The oaks were donated by the Queen for use by Reading Corporation to repair its nineteen bridges which were in poor condition when inherited from the Abbot by the Crown after the dissolution in 1539 and were transferred to the town by Queen Elizabeth. At the time of the Charter which gave him Whitley Park, Sir Francis Knollys (1515-1596) lived with his wife, Lady Catherine, at Grey's Court, near Henley, which had been given to him by King Henry VIII. He was already the owner of Caversham Park where he had built a grand manor house.

At the time of Henry VIII, before the Dissolution of Reading Abbey, the Manor of Whitley was stated as paying £26 18s 4d, Whitley Park was paying £3 and the rectory of Whitley was paying £20, all to the Abbey as tithes or taxes. There appears to be no record of where the rectory was.

The Manor of Whitley, as held after the 16th century, gradually extended to reach from just north of Southern Hill (now Christchurch Road), adjoining the Manor of Reading, to Whitley Wood Common in the south, adjoining Shinfield Manor. To the east it extended into what is now Whiteknights Park and most of Leighton Park and to the west it reached out to beyond the Kennet and Foudry Brook. As seen in the Introduction, John Doran's 'History of Reading' published in 1835 records the Beating of the Bounds of the Corporation of Reading taken in 1714, which shows the western extent of the Manor and Hamlet of Whitley as going beyond the western boundary of the Parish of St Giles in the Manor of Reading; it extends across the river Kennet for some distance until reaching the Holy Brook near the place where the Reading-Basingstoke Branch Line now passes south of Southcote.

Prior to the Beating of the Bounds, an earlier reference to the meadows around Whitley is in the 'Abstract of the Vachell Papers' held in the Reading Central Library and dated around 1630 in the reign of Charles I, which was when when the Vachell family took over most of the Manor of Whitley. Reference is made to Anmer's Mead, Vobney Mead and Small Mead. Vobney or Fobney Mead was opposite the old Rose Kiln leading down to where the old Sewage Farm used to be at Manor Farm. Small Mead was the land on the south of the river Kennet opposite Fobney Mead. Anmer's Mead may be the land where Searle's Farm is today, further west outside the bounds of the Manor of Whitley.

The Earl of Banbury, William Knollys, succeeded Sir Francis when he died in 1596. After being granted the Manor with the Park, the Earl sold off the Manor other than the Park to Sir William Whitmore and to George and Thomas Whitmore.

In 1627, the Park was sold to William Kendrick, brother of John Kendrick, who was the wealthy clothier that made his fortune in Reading, Oxford and then London after starting life in Reading and who died in 1624. The sale came about as a result of John Kendrick's will, whereby his younger brother William sold the family home in Minster Street to the Corporation to provide land for a workhouse and this became the Oracle workhouse. A legacy in the will was used to buy stock for loan to clothiers who employed the poor in the workhouse. With the proceeds from the sale of the property, William purchased Whitley Park manor house, an old Tudor building. Successive generations of Kendricks continued to live there until William's great-great granddaughter, Frances, inherited the estate in 1699 and then decided to move on to Calcot Park, where she died in 1722.

The location of the manor house is uncertain but it is believed to be where Whitley Park Farm House was later built, accessed from what became Whitley Park Lane and from Whitley Road (what is now Basingstoke Road). Nevertheless, the painting of Whitley Park Farm, shown on the front cover and held by the Museum of English Rural Life, shows a large house on the side of the hill, which could well be the later replacement for the Tudor manor house that had been occupied by the Kendrick families… but, there again, it could just be a separate Farm House! [Leslie North, writing in the Reading Chronicle in 1980, pored over this conundrum and was inconclusive too.]

The Vachell family then took over the Manor without the Park in 1629 (Sir Thomas Vachell had married the daughter of Sir Francis Knollys), as described in the abstract of the Vachell papers that were previously mentioned in this chapter. In the early 18th century, the Park was sold to Colonel Richard Thompson who was Sheriff of Berkshire around that time. He also owned Coley Park. By the 19th century, the Manor was recorded as being owned by Miss Frances Jennings (according to John Man in 1816 and then by J Robertson in 1843) and the Park was separately owned by Messrs. Allotson and Bros of London in 1843.

It appears that Messrs. Allotson & Bros put the entire 'Whitley Park Estate' up for sale in 1852 – a sale catalogue announcing this is held in the Reading Central Library. Certain parts were excluded, including the Four Horseshoes public house, the properties in Whitley Road to the King's Head Pond corner and along the Southern Hill to Whitley Park Lane. Some of the estate land was acquired for what was to be the Cintra estate by Thomas Newell and this passed to Martin Hope Sutton in 1857. In 1876, Richard Attenborough, a wealthy man with silversmith and pawnbroker businesses in London and living at 'Whitley Grove', is recorded as purchasing much of the Whitley Park estate. The whole of this estate, except for

Whitley Wood farm house and an adjacent field, was eventually acquired by Ann Whitworth during the 1870s and early 1880s. Then, in 1885, the title passed from Ann Whitworth to Samuel Palmer, brother of George Palmer, for £71,000. By 1893, he had acquired the remaining parts of Whitley Wood. In addition, he had acquired the ownership of the piece of land between Basingstoke Road and the river Kennet, bounded on the north by the Waterloo Kiln and on the south by the lane leading to the old Rose Kiln (now Rose Kiln Lane).

After Samuel's death in 1903, the Whitley Park Estate was put up for sale by his four sons (Ernest, Charles, Albert and Howard) and, though some was retained by his son Howard until well into the 20th century, much was acquired by the Reading Corporation. A significant proportion of the land was up for sale again in 1906 and also in 1926. During that time, the estate did not include a number of properties on the fringes, for example the Four Horseshoes Inn, the Long Barn, Whitley Rise, Whitley Lodge, Cintra Lodge estate, Christ Church with its glebe, Christchurch Gardens, the World Turned Upside Down and the Merry Maidens public houses, some plots in Whitley Wood (Common) Road, Whitley House and Whitley School. The land on the river side of Basingstoke Road was put up for sale in 1904. Following these sales, the development of the whole of Whitley started and, by the end of the 20th century, West Whitley out to the Kennet and Foudry Brook was becoming largely used for industrial and commercial businesses (the remainder still marsh and meadow land) and Central Whitley was used almost entirely for housing.

It is noted in Leslie Harman's 'Parish of St Giles-in-Reading' that there was a dispute over payment of tithes in 1716 for lands in Whitley that had been previously owned by William Kendrick. From 1633 William Kendrick had given an annual sum of 40s from lands called 'Councells' in Whitley for *maintaining the incumbent of the parish church, celebration of divine service and preaching the Holy Word*. This was intended to continue after William Kendrick's death. The lands had been Abbey lands and were tithe-free. Richard Watlington had owned a 'piddle of pasture' in 1596, south of a little lane to the west of Whitley Park and north of Councells, indicating that the land called Councells was just north-east of the Long Barn and the Four Horseshoes Inn and therefore that it was probably on the edge of what was later the Home Farm estate. The dispute raised by the then vicar of St Giles' turned out to be about whether the Watlington land was tithe-able or was part of Councells and therefore tithe-free. It was never resolved.

According to the sale catalogue of 1852, the Whitley Park Estate is described as *forming a respectable and commodious farm residence pleasantly placed on a dry elevated spot with good views and in the midst of grounds capable of being easily made very ornamental and surrounded by about 410 acres in a perfect ring fence lying opposite Whiteknights and Pepper Park Estates.* Thus it sits along Shinfield Road for much of its extent. The House is described as *approached by Private Road, with a neat octagon brick and slated entrance lodge from the Turnpike Road, contains four goods attics, four large bedrooms and a dressing room, a large parlour and common living room, kitchen, back kitchen or wash-house, dairy, pantry, cellars and a flower garden, walled in, with a summer house and a large productive kitchen garden, some out offices and a fine horse pond, etc.* There is also a farm homestead and yard, enclosed by a brick wall, with extensive farming facilities to the north and another homestead to the south. The land includes Marshall's Hill which was later to be the location of Cressingham Road.

The rest of the Whitley estate offered in the 1852 sale catalogue comprised five farms – Grey's, Wheatley, Curling's, Lovegrove's and Waterloo farms - and also cottages and meadows, some extending into the parish of Shinfield. The total estate comprised 840 acres, though this is not the entire Manor of Whitley as parts of the Manor had been leased for the building of houses particularly along Southern Hill and down Whitley Road and received a rental of around £1350. The farms were predominantly used for dairy farming as the land was most suited to this. Cattle were taken to and from the town's cattle market by droving them to Basingstoke Road and then along Katesgrove Lane.

The map on the next page shows the whole of Whitley around 1885 with its boundary, all the farms existing at that time and the main surrounding parkland. The main road in the centre is the Basingstoke road while the road on the right is the Shinfield road.

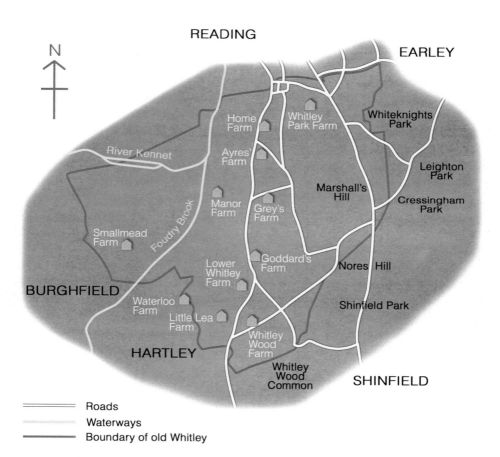

N

READING

EARLEY

Whiteknights
Park

Home
Farm

Whitley
Park Farm

River Kennet

Ayres
Farm

Leighton
Park

Marshall's
Hill

Cressingham
Park

Manor
Farm

Grey's
Farm

Foudry Brook

Smallmead
Farm

BURGHFIELD

Goddard's
Farm

Nores Hill

Lower
Whitley
Farm

Waterloo
Farm

Shinfield Park

Little Lea
Farm

HARTLEY

Whitley
Wood
Farm

Whitley
Wood
Common

SHINFIELD

Roads
Waterways
Boundary of old Whitley

Chapter 3

Development of the Hamlet and Manor of Whitley

The Manor of Whitley in the late 18th century was very sparsely populated, indeed there were only 28 people listed in the area in 1801. The One Mile marker from the town of Reading was close to the Four Horseshoes Inn on the Basingstoke Road while the Two Mile marker was close to the junction of Whitley Wood Lane with Basingstoke Road and the Three Mile marker was at Three Mile Cross (the latter being just outside the Manor of Whitley).

The land was all farm land, the names of most of the farms varying over time depending on the tenant farmer. Whitley Park Farm was accessed by a lane from Southern Hill on the Shinfield road, though the Park itself extended virtually the whole of the side of the hill down to Whitley Wood Common. Home Farm was just northeast of the Four Horseshoes Inn. Ayer's Farm was just southeast of the Four Horseshoes Inn. Grey's Farm was on the land around what is now Whitley Park School. Goddard's Farm was on the land in the area of what is now Hartland Road near Basingstoke Road. Whitley Wood Farm was by the junction of what is now Whitley Wood Road and Basingstoke Road. Little Lea Farm was close to Hartley Court on the west side of Basingstoke Road opposite Whitley Wood Farm. Whitley Manor Farm was on the opposite side of Basingstoke Road from Grey's Farm and close to the Foudry Brook. All the above farms, except Whitley Park Farm, were accessed from the Basingstoke Road, directly or via lanes. Small Mead Farm was just inside the western boundary while Waterloo Farm and Great Lea Farm were just outside Whitley on the western side.

Until the end of the 18th century, the main route through the Whitley farms was by use of the Long Barn lane which started from the Basingstoke road as now and ran through to meet Whitley Wood Common at the place where Northumberland Avenue joins Whitley Wood Road today. Other smaller lanes ran through the estate to provide access. The outer parts of Whitley were also uninhabited at that time, including the area along the northern side of Southern Hill from Whitley Street to Red Lane, which was later renamed Redlands Road, and the area along the Earley side of Shinfield Lane from Red Lane to Shinfield Green.

The name 'Southern Hill' was used not only to describe what is now Christchurch Road beyond Kendrick Road but it was also used to describe the area down Redlands Road, from Christchurch Road to Upper Redlands Road, and along Upper Redlands Road to the boundary of Whitley at Eastern Avenue. This included the area between Upper Redlands Road and Whiteknights Park. (The part of Christchurch Road between Kendrick Road and Whitley Street was known as Whitley Crescent and sometimes directories included it in Whitley Road). This generalised name for the area described has made it difficult to identify the locations of various places in the census listings, of course!

There were turnpikes in Whitley Street and in Red Lane near Southern Hill to control access between Reading and Whitley. Another turnpike was situated between 'The Elms', which was at the corner of Whitley Wood Road and Basingstoke Road, and the turning to Whitley Wood Common at this time, covering the boundary between Whitley and Shinfield (the Shinfield Gate). Also there was a pond on the corner of Whitley Street and Southern Hill, known as the King's Head Pond because it was close to the King's Head public house on the corner of Cut-throat Lane, to allow horses to quench their thirst after pulling coaches or carts up the hill either into town or away from town (and the occupants to quench their thirst in the King's Head, no doubt). This pond would have been fed from the hill's spring water.

So, as the years moved forward from the 18th century, Whitley was very much farm land with virtually no population, save for the tenant farmers in the farm houses and the agricultural labourers living in the tied cottages associated with the farms, and it had changed little in structure since the Middle Ages. However, the bordering areas started to develop in the early part of the 19th century and so the population started to grow. This came with the development of large-scale industries in the town and new wealth being created, resulting in heavy demand for new housing along the top of Southern Hill and down Whitley Road.

The first development along Southern Hill was a terrace of fifteen houses built at the west end, close to the King's Head pond, probably in the 1820s, and known as Whitley Crescent. Also a villa house, called Whitley Villa, was built on the corner opposite the pond and next to the terrace. It was not until about 1887 that a sixteenth house (Christchurch Cottage) was added to the terrace at the west end where the Villa's stable yard had stood. Mrs Slocombe, who owned the Whitley Villa, moved from there into Christchurch Cottage when it was completed. Whitley Villa and the original fifteen houses are probably the oldest set of buildings still in existence in Whitley – even the 'Four Horseshoes

Inn' (now demolished) was rebuilt much later, in the mid-20th century. It is interesting to note that, listed in the 1841 census, the ninth house in Whitley Crescent at that time (now No 21 Christchurch Road), was the home of Joseph Huntley, original founder of the Huntley (and Palmer) biscuit-making business and the Huntley (Boorne and Stevens) tin-making business; this was after his retirement from the business and a few years before his death in 1849. Other houses in the terrace were occupied by a schoolmistress, a clergyman, a professor and other professional people.

The photograph below, taken in 2016, shows Whitley Villa to the left (for many years it has been a doctor's surgery) and then the sixteen houses in the Whitley Crescent terrace .

Of course, the 1841 census also listed the other residents in the area at that time. Whitley was divided into two parts for census purposes. It described the area west of the Basingstoke/Southampton turnpike road as 'West Whitley' and that description has been kept for the purposes of this book. The area to the east of that road (including the Shinfield turnpike road) is described there as 'East Whitley'. However, for this book, it is described as 'Central Whitley' between Basingstoke Road and the Shinfield Road and as 'East Whitley' only for the part beyond the Shinfield Road.

On the western side of the hill on the road to Basingstoke, Colonel Everett, a wool draper, and his family lived with their governess in a large house and also another gentleman and his wife lived in a house along that road. Many labourers and their families had cottages as did a blacksmith and family, and a schoolmistress, a shopkeeper and a carpenter. There were three farmers who apparently managed the Waterloo Farm, the Little Lea Farm and the Great Lea Farm. Mr Billings' Kiln was listed, which probably would have been the Rose Kiln as later named.

On the eastern side of Basingstoke Road, it was much more varied. Apart from information about Whitley Crescent and Whitley Villa, there were Whitley Park Farm, Gray's Farm, Curling's Farm, Pippeard Farm (run by the Goddard family) and Whitley Wood Farm. Each farm had several tied cottages associated with them. There were quite a few houses and cottages along Southern Hill, together with the 'Wheel' beer shop and the 'John Bull' beer shop. One cottage included a schoolmaster and 16 children with servants. Down Whitley Road on the hill was Whitley Cottage. The Whiteknights turnpike and gatekeeper are listed together with three associated cottages. The Four Horseshoes public house and the six Long Barn cottages at the rear are also listed, together with the 'World Turned Upside Down' beer shop (later to be a public house), the Shinfield Gate and also several cottages in Back Lane (probably the early name for part of Whitley Wood Road).

An early building of The Four Horseshoes public house in Basingstoke Road, c.1870, is shown in the photograph below. The hanging sign over the door shows four horseshoes and the sign board has the name of the landlord,

Charles Ransom, who was there for many years. In the foreground is a pair of horses together with a horse and cart. Behind the public house the Long Barn cottages can be seen.

Altogether there were 99 people listed to the west and 410 to the east making a total of 509 people registered in Whitley in the 1841 census.

1840s

During the 1840s, a number of additional properties were built in Whitley Road on the hill, including 'Whitley House', 'Whitley Lodge', 'Kenilworth Cottage' and two pairs of houses at 'Whitley Place' (still existing at 64-70 Basingstoke Road), together with the 'Grenadier' beer house near Whitley Wood, later to become 'The Grenadier' public house.

Whitley Place is shown as it is today in this photograph. The four houses are very little changed in structure though some more modern facilities have been added.

1850s

Further development of the Whitley Hill area and Southern Hill was taking place, particularly with large estate properties. Thomas Huntley, of the Huntley and Palmer biscuit company, was living at the newly-built large house called 'Whitley Grove', which was situated below Milman Road on the side of Whitley Road. It was most likely that it was built for him. However, he died in 1857 and the property was taken over by Richard Attenborough, the gentleman who later purchased the Whitley Park estate. On the other side of Whitley Road was another newly-built large property known as 'Whitley Rise' that was occupied by Mr Alex Thwaites and then in the 1860s by J H Wilson, the Recorder for Henley, (a circuit judge).

In the same period, a number of significant new houses were constructed for the gentry. 'Cintra Lodge', with a large estate on one side of Southern Hill, was built for Thomas Newell and acquired by Martin Hope Sutton of Suttons Seeds shortly afterwards. 'Sutherlands' was built for William Silver Darter on the other side of Southern Hill (he had previously lived at 'Swiss Villa' in Kings Road). Next to Cintra Lodge was 'Ashton Lodge' erected for Lady Henrietta St Maur, listed in the 1861 census as "the daughter of a Duke". Next to Ashton Lodge was another new property, 'Merton House', built to house the Curate (and later Vicar) of St John's Church, William Payne.

Next to Merton House, Glenmore House was erected (this was later the location of Jarvis' Garage, which became a Peugeot dealership in the late 20th century before being transformed much more recently into Cintra Close). The 'Queen's Head' public house was built on the corner of the lane leading to the Whitley Park Farm. Meanwhile a School House for the Hamlet of Whitley School was listed on the hill nearer Whitley Street.

In East Whitley, 'Park House' was built further along the hill on the side of Whiteknights Park in Upper Redlands Road. Commander Thomas Birch of the Royal Navy was its first owner. 'Whiteknights House' and 'Blandford Lodge' were built in the 1850s in Whiteknights Park, within the bounds of East Whitley. Four other houses existed or were built in the Earley part of the Park.

In the early part of the 20th century, Edward Jackson, owner of the Jackson's department store, lived at Park House. The image below shows wounded soldiers of the Great War enjoying his hospitality in his garden in 1916. Most are seated on folding chairs while Mr Jackson stands by one of the tables facing the camera.

These were the first examples of the establishment of substantial properties along Southern Hill whereas previously they had been built in the main along the London Road and Kings Road area. There were, of course, many tradesmen living in cottages along Southern Hill as well, e.g. blacksmiths, wheelwrights, builders and market gardeners (all needed in support of the increasing number of properties in this area). To the west of Basingstoke Road, the Rose Kiln had opened close to the Kennet with John Wood being the brick-maker, one of the suppliers of bricks for the building of the large properties. Meanwhile Whitley Park Farm and the many other farms across the Whitley estate continued to make good use of the arable land for dairy and poultry produce together with fruit and vegetables.

There were more public houses appearing to meet the needs of the growing population - near the Redlands Road end of Southern Hill was the 'Robin Hood' public house and opposite Manor Farm Lane on Basingstoke Road was the 'World Turned Upside Down' public house. 'The Maidens Inn' in Shinfield Lane also appeared on the census in 1861.

1860s

One of the main developments was the building of Christ Church on Southern Hill, to a design by Henry Woodyer, such that it was facing down Kendrick Road to the north and also down the lane leading into the farm land of Whitley to the south. This was built in chapel style during 1861/2 and consecrated in August 1862. It was then extended in 1874, with a tower and spire added. A vicarage was built at the rear in 1871/2, to a design by Alfred Waterhouse, in what became called Vicarage Road.

The Lower Whitley School house in Whitley Wood had been opened in 1860 at the junction of Whitley Wood Lane and Basingstoke Road to provide Sunday School for the farm cottage children. However it soon became a local church house as part of the Christ Church parish.

At this time many farms were still listed in the Whitley basin. There were Whitley Park Farm, Home Farm (also known as Gully Farm, probably because of its location in a gully down Whitley Road hill), Manor Farm, Gray's Farm, Little Lea Farm, Rose Farm (which became known as Longbarn Farm and then later still Ayres' Farm), Back Lane Farm (Whitley Wood Farm) and Gulley Farm (in Whitley Wood, later called Lower Whitley Farm). Four cottages, known as

Dalkeith Cottages, were built near what had now become the Grenadier Inn. There were also many Whitley Cottages, used predominantly by farm labourers.

Christchurch Gardens was started in the 1860s with two houses (which were later numbered Nos. 8 and 10), and then No. 12 was built in 1878, all three properties being designed by Joseph Morris for Richard Attenborough of Whitley Grove, who owned the estate. By 1890, there were a total of 6 houses on the south side of the Gardens. Nos. 2, 4 and 6 Christchurch Gardens had been later additions and by the end of the century, Church Road had been opened up through the glebe land to the west of Christ Church as a link between Christchurch Road and Christchurch Gardens. This allowed further houses to be built in the late Victorian style on the three sides of the square bordered by Christchurch Road, Christchurch Gardens and Church Road (which soon became known as Glebe Road) to form a new area for housing some of the growing number of people in this part of Whitley.

Other changes in this period were a reservoir for the Water Works being constructed in the surrounding estate of William Silver Darter's house 'Sutherlands', Leighton Park being developed by Alexander Cobham and Cressingham Park being developed by the Lonergan family. Various cottages were erected in what was then called (and still is) New Road, which sits between Redlands Road and Upper Redlands Road.

'The Maidens' public house became known as 'The Merry Maidens' and 'The Sportsman' public house was built.

1870s and 1880s

Many additional houses were built in the 1870s and 1880s along Southern Hill, the fringes of Whiteknights Park and along the Shinfield Road but the heart of Whitley (the Central Whitley lower level and the West of Whitley near to the Kennet flood plain) remained predominantly farm land with farm houses and labourers' cottages.

The small estate of stylish houses called 'The Mount' was constructed in this period along Southern Hill (Christchurch Road). Mildmay Cottage was built between the Sutherlands estate and The Mount estate.

The photograph above shows the central part of The Mount estate and on the far left can just be seen the front entrance to the Progress Theatre.

Elmhurst house was built in Upper Redlands Road. The Royal Albert Job and Post House was opened next door to The Queen's Head. Along the side of The Queen's Head, a row of 5 terraced cottages, probably for the farm's agricultural workers, were erected along the lane leading to Whitley Park Farm and these became known as the Whitley Park Lane cottages.

The following photograph shows the Queen's Head public house with the distinctive impression of Queen Victoria's head on the left hand corner. To the right are very old painted signs for 'Royal Albert Garage, Proprietors: G Jarvis and Sons' on one wall and 'Cars, Coaches, Repairs' on the adjacent wall – these date back to the beginning of the 20th century.

The census for 1881 shows the number of houses in Whitley had significantly increased during the previous decade to some 250 and the population had increased from 952 to 1324 people. That was a doubling of the population compared with 130 houses and 639 people thirty years previously.

In response to rapid growth of the town, a Reading Borough boundary extension was permitted under the Reading Corporation Act of 1887 and the whole of Whitley was taken under the town's administration, facilitated by the completion of the sewage farm at Manor Farm. This enabled a range of services provided by the Borough to be extended to Whitley and to other districts that were brought into the town at the same time. In 1888, the town was renamed the County Borough of Reading.

Developments after the 1887 boundary changes up to the turn of the century

When Whitley was taken into the Borough of Reading, it was the start of a new phase of development of the estate. Where Brighton Terrace had been built in Katesgrove by the northern corner of Milman Road at the end of Whitley Street in 1883, two additional terraces were built between Milman Road and

Swainstone Road along Whitley Road in 1888 (St Leonard's Terrace of eight houses) and in 1900 (Weymouth Terrace of six houses). In between these two blocks there were already a few cottages that had been built a year or so earlier – Peacock Cottage to the north and the semi-detached Derby Cottages to the south with a narrow road between them - and the terrace blocks were constructed to abut them on either side.

Another terrace block had been built in the early 1890s to the south of Swainstone Road (the Swainstone Terrace) on land acquired from the Whitley Grove estate. Swainstone Road itself had also been developed with a row of terraced houses along its south side abutting the Whitley Grove estate. Further terrace blocks (the five-house Fair View Terrace and the thirteen-house Norfolk Terrace) were also built on Whitley Road/Basingstoke Road around 1890 to meet the increasing demand for housing as land from the Whitley Grove estate became available for development. A small group of houses (Rowley Road, Shenstone Road and Hagley Road) was built just north of Elgar Road (which had been cut through to the Waterloo Kiln by 1900), and then, during the period up to 1925 (when the remaining Whitley Grove estate was put up for sale), Clent Road was started. Further development during the 1930s and 40s saw the estate completely turned over for housing, Bourne Avenue was constructed on the land where Whitley Grove house had once stood, joining through to Hagley Road, and Clent Road was completed.

Former Highgrove House land on the corner of Kendrick Road and Christchurch Road was developed in 1896/7 by William Poulton, owner of the Waterloo Brick and Tile Works, with two large semi-detached houses (Kendrick Rise and Dryburgh) at Nos. 117 and 119 Kendrick Road, two large semi-detached houses on the corner at Nos. 35 and 37 Christchurch Road and a detached house,

(Hillingdon), at No 39 Christchurch Road. A stable block was erected in the grounds of 'Hillingdon' at the rear. William Poulton lived in 'Hillingdon' and his son Francis lived at No 41 next door which had been built at the west end of the 'Sutherlands' estate. Hillingdon was later used by the Milk Marketing Board before it was converted into a hotel, the 'Hillingdon Prince Hotel'. No 117 Kendrick Road was also developed as a hotel in the 1970s, the 'Sheringham Hotel', which together with No 119 was later (after the year 2000) added to the Hillingdon Prince as an annexe.

The photograph on the previous page shows the Hillingdon Prince Hotel with an added conservatory at the left side. On the gate post to the left the original 'Hillingdon' sign still exists in the brickwork.

So, by the 1901 census, Southern Hill (which by then was known as Christchurch Road) and Whitley Road (which by then had been absorbed into Basingstoke Road), were both becoming well developed. Some building had taken place in the part by and within Whiteknights Park – more cottages were erected in New Road as well as houses in Upper Redlands Road and Marlborough Avenue. John Heelas (of the large department store, Heelas and Sons, in the town) was living at Whiteknights House and the widow of Captain Miller, Marie, was living at Blandford Lodge with her family. Pepper Manor became Leighton Park and the present School had been opened there in 1890. Cressingham House and The Elms had been built on the Earley side of Shinfield Road with the Goodrest estate and the Shinfield Park estate standing on the Shinfield side of the Whitley estate. George Jarvis had taken over as the Royal Albert Job Master and opened his Royal Albert Garage coach (and later car) repair business there. Somerleaze House had been built for William Silver Darter and was later renamed Kensington House.

479. Christchurch Rd Reading.

The Christchurch Green shops, shown here, are the original group of shops built shortly before 1910 when this photograph was taken. There are only three gable fronted buildings shown – another six were added a few years later.

In 1901 the total number of houses had increased to nearly 400 and there were nearly 2000 people living in Whitley, a trebling of both figures in fifty years. As stated earlier, the vast majority of the Whitley estate was owned by the Palmer family and the Sutton family. The next fifty years would see another significant increase as the Whitley Park estate owned by these two families was sold off and developed for housing, both private and Council. By 1931, the total population of Whitley (Christ Church) parish had increased even further to 11,771, an enormous growth, leaving it as the largest parish in Southern Reading at that time compared with St Giles (9026), St Luke (4279), St John (5391) and St Bartholomew (7028).

The map on the next page shows the north of Whitley around 1900. It extends from Basingstoke Road and Whitley Road on the left to Shinfield Road and Whiteknights Park on the right. All the main Victorian houses of the time are indicated here.

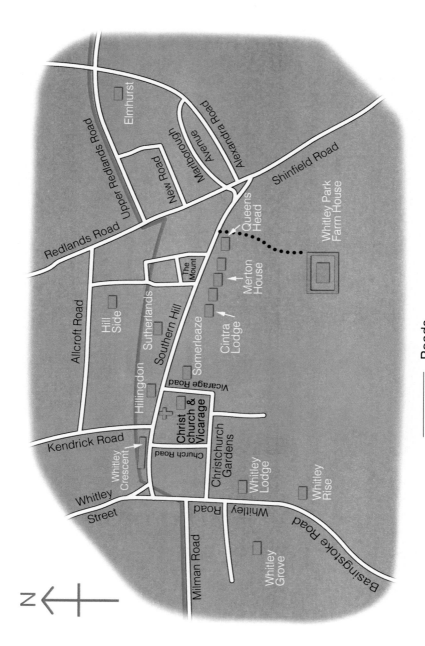

Roads
Boundary of old Whitley

Into the 20th century

In the first decade of the new century, a housing development was started along the eastern side of Whitley Park Farm for private ownership and was called Northcourt Avenue, the first significant build on former Whitley farm land. Building of private houses gradually continued along the east side of Basingstoke Road down the hill together with the opening up of the George Palmer Schools. It also started down a newly-developed Northumberland Avenue, including the Whitley Special School that was built to meet the special educational needs of the children of the town.

Below is a scene in Northcourt Avenue around 1930. The view takes the eye along to the junction with Wellington Avenue on the left while Northcourt Avenue bends to the right. It is interesting to note the unmade road and footpath, the high electricity poles and the street gas lamp.

The start of the Great War in 1914 meant significant disruption to the town in general and to schools, the hospital and local industries in particular. Some of the schools were requisitioned to provide extra accommodation for hospital use in addition to the hundreds of beds provided at the Royal Berkshire Hospital. At the George Palmer centre workshops, 70 out of 120 boys over the age of 13 showed remarkable skill and they volunteered to give up Wednesday evening and Saturday morning to work. Using material from the Reading War Hospitals Supplies Depot, the centre made metal fittings for splints, wooden bandage winders, metal arm cradles and body and leg cradles. The George Palmer centre is shown in the following photograph (taken during the Great War) where the boys can be seen making various parts for appliances.

During the inter-war years, there were new housing estates developed with the first council housing estate begun in 1920 along the western side of Shinfield Road and then a large council estate in Central Whitley was started in 1931. Many of the old large family estates, including the large houses, became difficult to maintain and started to become run down, so the land was sold off for development and this assisted the growth of the new housing estates or, in many cases, the houses were converted into flats.

Up to the Second World War, just out of Whitley beyond Whitley Wood Road was the Shinfield Park estate that included Goodrest as well as properties like The Grove and Shinfield Lodge. During the War, the land was requisitioned for RAF use and that continued until well after 1945 when the War ended.

Reading became the post-War regional administrative centre for the Government using large houses and buildings that were available to be requisitioned. This included buildings along Christchurch Road. At the time of the Coronation of Queen Elizabeth II in June 1953, beacons were set up on high points around the town, including one at the top of Cressingham Road, and street parties were held across the area.

After the austerity of the post-war Fifties, the combination of big demand for housing and the growth of light industries and then service industries led to an almost complete use of the land across Whitley. Thus began a new period of growth and change in the town and especially in Whitley. The development of housing estates in several parts of the town – Tilehurst, Southcote, for example, as well as Whitley - was primarily to address the growing council housing list, especially resulting from the baby boom of that period, and the need for redevelopment of older housing in other parts of the town. This was a major activity once the housing controls had receded and raw materials were flowing again. The Whitley estate expanded out to fill the whole of Central Whitley, from Basingstoke Road to Shinfield Road and from Christchurch Road to Whitley Wood, and this heralded the rapid demise of the farming tradition of the parish. Meanwhile, on the other side of Basingstoke Road, a large commercial and industrial estate started to emerge.

A new sewage works was opened at Manor Farm in Whitley in 1963. This £2m development was intended to improve the capability to manage the town's effluent for the rest of the century. However, it transpired that the works generated a smell on various occasions which penetrated the south of Reading under a prevailing westerly wind or even into the town itself. This became known locally as the 'Whitley Whiff'! It was not until the turn of the century that this problem was finally overcome despite many attempts and promises of success in between.

Conservation Areas were introduced in Reading in the 1980s to try and prevent more fine buildings in the town from coming under threat of demolition as a result of developments like the Inner Distribution Road. The third and fourth of these designated areas were the Christchurch Conservation Area and The Mount Conservation Area, both in 1987.

The Christchurch Conservation Area covers Christ Church, the old and new vicarages, Abbey Junior School (Kensington House), Christchurch Road from 1-33 (Whitley Crescent) and 35-49 together with the 'Hillingdon Prince Hotel' site at 117-119 Kendrick Road and the entire area bounded by Christchurch Gardens, Glebe Road, Whitley Street and Christchurch Road.

The Mount Conservation Area covers The Mount estate itself, Progress Theatre, 53 and 53A Christchurch Road (part of the old Sutherlands estate), 55 Christchurch Road (Mildmay Cottage) and also Hillside in Allcroft Road.

There are several listed buildings in Whitley and some are included in these Conservation Areas:

Christ Church itself is Grade II* listed.

The rest of the following are Grade II listed:

Christ Church Vicarage
St Paul's former Church Hall (now cottages)
'Whitley Place' houses at 64-70 Basingstoke Road
'Whitley Villa' and 'Whitley Crescent' at 1-33 Christchurch Road
The Victorian houses of 'The Mount' and at 85-89 Christchurch Road
Whiteknights Park House lodge at 31 Shinfield Road
Leighton Park School's original school house
'Old Whiteknights House'
'Blandford Lodge'.
The hexagonal building at 11 Elmhurst Road.

Chapter 4

Significant Properties in Victorian Whitley

This chapter provides some background information on several of the large houses built in the north of Whitley during the 19th century.

Whitley Lodge. In 1843, a prominent landowner of the time, Thomas Owst, occupied this property, which was near the Whitley boundary at the top of Whitley Road. He was at one time the owner of Hartley Court and Shinfield Manor (see Chapter 1). In 1875 it was acquired by Captain Austen - his family continued to own it after his death in the late 1880s. His wife was the owner until at least the start of the Great War. During the 1920s the house was used as a school that was run by Miss Linay. The Whitley Lodge continued to exist well into the 20th century.

Whitley Rise. This was a large house, halfway down Whitley Hill, with coach house and gardener's cottage in the grounds, which was built in the 1850s and was occupied by Mr Alex Thwaites. Then, in the 1860s, it was owned by J H Wilson, Recorder for Henley, followed by Charles Stevens in the 1880s. Around 1900, Col. H D Buchanan-Dunlop took over the property. During the Second War he allowed the property to be used by the Civil Defence.

By 1952, it was used by Reading Technical College and, although it was still owned by the Buchanan-Dunlop family, Whitley Rise was made available to the Education Committee for use by George Palmer Central School as an Annexe in the 1940s and 1950s. The coach house was used by the Building Department for practising brick-laying and other skills and the house was also used by the Avenue School. Air Raid shelters were erected for use by school children during the Second World War and the younger pupils went there for Air Raid drills. In the 1950s it was demolished to make way for a major extension to the Avenue School, leaving the coach house and the cottage intact. When the Avenue School was demolished in 2009/10, the remaining Whitley Rise buildings went as well. The name, Whitley Rise, was revived for the road that gives access from Basingstoke Road to the replacement Care Home.

Whitley Grove. This was built for Thomas Huntley (of the biscuit company) probably around 1856 but he died the following year and Richard Attenborough acquired the estate. The property was well positioned on the side of Whitley Hill facing down to the Kennet. The estate of some 100 acres comprised a large house on the hill with a southerly and westerly outlook and was accessed through a wooded area from Whitley Road via a long drive guarded by an entrance lodge. The estate extended down Whitley hill from what is now Swainstone Road and then to the west unbroken to the river Kennet. It was unbroken because Katesgrove Lane did not cut through to the Basingstoke Road at that time but ended at the Katesgrove Kiln. The only part not owned by the estate was that occupied on Whitley Road by the Whitley Place houses and their gardens. It did however include the Waterloo Brick and Tile Kiln property and a farm and park land. William Poulton, who ran the Waterloo Kiln for many years, was also the tenant farmer at the Whitley Grove Farm for a while. The southerly direction from the house looked out over Whitley farm lands to Whitley Wood while the westerly direction looked out over the Kennet basin and across to Coley Park and Southcote manor.

The estate was then sold in the mid-1880s to John Egginton (an estate agent in the town) after Richard Attenborough's death in 1881 at the age of 61. By the mid-1890s, Walter May, whose family owned the St Giles' Mill, had acquired the estate. Gradually parts of it were sold off and at the turn of the century a small group of houses was constructed to form Hagley Road, Rowley Road and Shenstone Road. Elgar Road, a change of name from Katesgrove Lane for this section of road had been cut through from Basingstoke Road to the Waterloo Kiln. Then sale of the estate in 1925, following the death of Walter's son, Herbert May, released the remainder of the land and house for gradual development. In that sale, the property was described as a family residence with outbuildings, tennis and croquet lawns, a well-stocked kitchen garden and small paddock together with stabling, a coach house, another kitchen garden and paddock, and also a timbered area suitable for building to the north and east.

Sutherlands. William Silver Darter, one-time Mayor of Reading moved to this newly-built house from Swiss Villa in King's Road in the 1840s, at the time when he ran his Lead and Glass Merchant business in London Street. He moved in the mid-1870s to another new house, Somerleaze, in Southern Hill. By 1900, Sutherlands house was occupied by Mrs Breedon and the western lodge house, next door to 'Hillingdon', was used by the gardener. On the eastern boundary of the Sutherlands estate was a second lodge house and a large coach house and stables, both of which were adjacent to the Reading Water Works reservoir – no longer there - which fed some of the Southern Hill community. Part of the land (the western half) was sold and the western lodge became an independent house, which was later occupied by Francis Poulton. Another part of the land was used to create the private road, Sutherlands Avenue, adjacent to the western lodge house and additional houses were built along Christchurch Road.

After the Great War, Sutherlands was used as a Hostel for Wounded Soldiers and then, in 1923, the house with its remaining property was put up for sale and was described as having a hall, large drawing room, dining room, morning room, billiards room, eleven bedrooms, three bathrooms, a lodge, stabling and garage in two acres of land. Around 1930, the house was used as the No IX School. Later the property was owned by the Sutton family and occupied by Leonard Noel Sutton (titled Major after the Second World War). After his widow died, the house was demolished and replaced with a new modern 'Sutherlands' in the 1970s that had been built nearer to the Christchurch Road while the remaining land was sold for development as the Lancaster Close estate. The eastern lodge house and the coach house still stand, though the reservoir has long gone.

To the east of Sutherlands, between the reservoir and The Mount estate, was a footpath which led from Christchurch Road around Hillside House and out onto Allcroft Road – this route was reputed to have been used by Martin Hope Sutton of Cintra Lodge to walk to the Suttons Seeds premises while talking with his good friend, George Palmer, who lived at the Acacias and walked to the Kings Road biscuit factory. The footpath became known as Sutton's Walk and the name was given to the small estate of dwellings built on the site of the path, adjacent to Hillside House.

Cintra Lodge. This property on Southern Hill had a long and varied history until its demise in the 1950s. The house was built early in the 1850s for Thomas Newell and, following his death, the estate was sold to Martin Hope Sutton (of the Suttons Seeds family) in 1857. The property was described as an *elegant, modern Villa Residence, built in Italian style with a large walled-in Garden well planted and tastefully laid out with lawn, flower beds and choice shrubs in front, kitchen garden at the rear. The estate is of an Acre and one quarter*. A lodge house was sited at the western entrance and this still exists as a private house.

Martin Hope Sutton owned Cintra Lodge and its land until his death in 1903, when the whole estate was sold. A fuller description of the house was given in the sale details – *a detached and commodious Family Residence, situate in delightful and well-matured grounds*. The house comprised two small rooms in the tower and eight bedrooms on the first floor with a spacious landing and W.C. The Dining Room, Drawing Room, Morning Room, Study, Conservatory and Balcony, Housekeeper's Room, 2 bedrooms and W.C. were on the ground floor. In the basement were the kitchen, scullery, and servant's quarters. There were two vineries, four greenhouses, etc. and a small farmery of cowhouse, stable and outbuildings.

This photograph shows Cintra Lodge from the rear with Ashton Lodge (now Phoenix College) in the background. The building is heavily covered in climbing plants. The date of the photograph is unknown and it is unclear whether the property was occupied at the time either by a resident or for educational purposes but it does look somewhat overgrown.

Between 1857 and 1903, an adjoining estate had been established and had grown significantly as M. H. Sutton had acquired some 24 and a half acres of park land from various landowners including William Silver Darter, Richard Attenborough and Walter May. This extra land was offered for sale as part of the whole Cintra Lodge estate for use as building land, because it was on a bed of *excellent gravel, in itself of great local value* and plans were offered for its development. However that did not happen and, fortunately, that land was retained as a public park, now known as Cintra Park Recreation Ground.

Between 1909 and 1917 the house with its garden was used by Abbey School as a residence for its boarders. From 1917 until the Second World War, it was used by the University as a women's residential student hall, later named Ashdown Hall. After the Second World War, the building was occupied by the Ministry of Labour and National Service and was then demolished in the 1950s.

The name Cintra, which has variously been applied to a Park, a School, and most recently to a Close, is most likely to have been used as an anglicised version of Sintra, the name of a Moorish Castle in Portugal, which was restored in the early 19th century – whether Thomas Newell had visited the place we do not know.

Ashton Lodge. This house on Southern Hill was built for Lady Henrietta St Maur (originally Seymour). She was the fourth daughter and fifth of seven children from the first marriage of Sir Edward Adolphus St Maur, 11th Duke of Somerset (Duke Street was named after his Tudor ancestor, the Lord Protector). Lady Henrietta was born in 1810 and moved into Ashton Lodge in the late 1850s, around the same time that Cintra Lodge was built. She died in 1890 without having any children. The house was then owned by Henry Wallis JP, a corn and seed merchant, until the 1920s. During the Second World War and afterwards, the house was occupied by the Ministry of Agriculture Fisheries and Food and also the Regional Office of the National Savings Committee. This continued until the house was taken over in 1957 by the Reading Borough Training Centre for mentally-handicapped children and was renamed as Wakefield Lodge. With some variation in the focus of the school the name was later changed through Reading Alternative School to the present-day Phoenix College.

Merton House. Next to Ashton Lodge, this was built in the 1850s and was occupied initially by William Payne, the curate of St John's Church, who lived there with his family. By the Great War, it was occupied by his widow, Mrs Payne, and then in 1921 it was operated as a Private Hotel. In 1949, the house was being used as a school for boys. The house was finally demolished in the 1950s and replaced with a block of residences called Morton Court which still exist today.

Somerleaze House. William Silver Darter had this house built for himself and his family, on Southern Hill close to Christ Church, around 1876 to a design by Alfred Waterhouse. He moved there from Sutherlands, nearby on the other side of the road. After he died in 1897, it was acquired by Samuel Wheeler and it is understood that it was renamed Hatch Gate and then by the 1920s named Horton Lodge, in which Rev. Trotter lived. The house, finally named Kensington House and having been extended, was put up for sale by the trustees of Samuel Wheeler in 1945. It was described as containing a lounge, hall, 3 large reception rooms, a billiards room, ten bedrooms, two bathrooms, four W.C.s, domestic offices, outbuildings, large garage and excellent gardens occupying about an acre. The house was built of blue Staffordshire brick with white brick facings and a slated roof.

At the end of the Second World War, Kensington House was acquired by the Abbey School for its Junior School and it remains there today, though it had been used previously in the 1920s as temporary accommodation for Abbey School boarders. The name Somerleaze House was revived for an annexe built in 2006 adjacent to the School and this followed the building of a substantial extension to the main house for the Junior School some years earlier.

The colouring of the brickwork and the Waterhouse design of the house can still be seen today as in the above photograph taken in 2017. To the extreme right are the extension and the associated outbuilding erected around the end of the 20th century for the Abbey Junior School.

Whitley Glebe. At the corner of Christchurch Gardens and the east side of Glebe Road, this was built for Montagu Wheeler around 1900. After the Great War, two of the Sutton sisters, Jessie and Florence, lived here. In the late 20th century, the house was taken over by Synexus, a medical research company running clinical trials. It vacated the property some years later and ARCADE (Amethyst Resource Centre for Alcohol and Drug Education) established its own centre there to support various related projects. ARCADE had been running these projects since 1994. Amethyst (a charitable temperance organisation) was established in 1832 and had been well known at Palmer Hall in Reading's West Street over many decades. In October 2013, ARCADE also set up a new faith school, the independent Trinity Christian School, which started with just two pupils, the teachers being drawn from local Christian church groups. It was intended to attract a small number of pupils from 4 to 11 years and, in 2016, there were eight pupils in attendance.

Whiteknights House was built as a family home for Alfred Waterhouse Senior and his wife Mary in 1858. They had been attracted from Liverpool (where Alfred Senior had been a cotton broker) by the Quaker ties already established in the area – Huntley and Palmers, Simonds brewery, Suttons Seeds, etc. The house was built to a design of

Charles Smith, a prominent local architect. It was further enhanced by their son, Alfred Waterhouse Junior, the renowned Victorian architect, in 1861/2 and it continued to be their family home until the death of Alfred Senior in 1875 and then his wife Mary in 1880. A lodge for the house was built in 1882 at the Shinfield Road entrance to the Park at the end of Chancellor's Way and was called Whiteknights Park Lodge.

For many years Whiteknights House was the home of John Heelas, a founder and chairman of Heelas, Sons and Co. He died there in 1910 at the age of 84, leaving his son, John Heelas Junior, as the only survivor of his six children. This photo shows him in his later years, at which time his granddaughter, Katherine Pearce Gould, lived with him and looked after his household for him.

The Whiteknights House estate then passed to others before being acquired by Max Railing of the General Electric Company. He lived there with his family and was a relative and colleague of Hugo Hirst, the head of GEC, who had taken residence at Foxhill House nearby. Railing was expected to take over from Hirst as head of GEC but died a year before Hirst in 1942. Railing's family continued to live at Whiteknights House until the lease ran out following the purchase of the Park by the University in 1947.

In 1952, the house was used by the University as the first proper home for the Museum of English Rural Life following its creation in the 1940s. Whiteknights House later became the home for the School of Law until its move to Foxhill House in the Park in 2004. From then it has been the home for the Graduate School of the Arts and Humanities Faculty. In more recent times, the house has been known as 'Old Whiteknights House' so as to differentiate it from the new administration building next door which was given the name of 'Whiteknights House'.

Blandford Lodge was in existence in 1862 when Charles Smith, the local architect, was commissioned to design and carry out alterations to 'Blandford

House'. There has been no evidence of the actual date of its original design and build. It was probably named after, and may have been built for, the Marquis of Blandford, owner of Whiteknights Park earlier that century. The additions were done for George Oataker, presumably a lessee of the house and grounds from the Goldsmid family who owned the Park at that time. Charles Smith carried out further alterations to the house in 1867, the year that the Park was divided into six leaseholds of which Blandford House (recorded as Lodge in the deeds for the lease) was on one of the estates. Charles Easton was the lessee taking on the house at that time; he was also owner of the Whiteknights Park House lease and manager of the whole Park Estate for the Goldsmid family. A new small lodge was built for Charles Easton's house on the estate to the design of his friend Charles Smith in 1868, though this no longer exists. From that time, the building was known as Blandford Lodge. The walls of the present adjoining car park on the north side are the original walls of the Lodge's garden. Mrs Shafto was the lessee during the 1870s. In 1893, Henry Jagoe lived there followed by Captain Miller in 1899. After he died, his widow, Marie, continued to live there with her family for several years. Later, in the 20th century, the house was used as an annexe to Whiteknights Park House for student accommodation. More recently, it has been in use as an administration building.

This photograph shows the Lodge around 1890 when it was a private residence. It looks very different now. It is interesting to note the croquet hoops set out on the back lawn, the conservatory to the left, the two figures sat in the open French window and the outside of the house covered with climbing plants.

Park House was situated in Upper Redlands Road in East Whitley, the three acre estate being opposite the land on which Broad Oak (now part of St Joseph's College) was later built. This estate was sub-leased by Charles Easton to Captain Thomas Birch on a 99-year lease at around 1860. Having lived there since around 1851, Captain Birch and his family and then, after his death, his widow Ann were resident in the property until the first decade of the 20th century. After Ann Birch's death at the age of 90 in 1906, Edward Jackson (1850-1928) took over the sub-lease. Mr Jackson was Chairman of the Jackson's store at Jackson's Corner (Market Place/King's Road) in the town centre and also a J.P. He was Mayor of Reading in 1905. He continued living at Park House until his death in 1928 in his late 70s. (Edward Jackson is shown in a photograph taken at Park House in Chapter 3). By 1930, M. Audley Fouquet Sutton was occupying the property and, in due course, its freehold was acquired by the University. It was used for a few years by the National Savings Committee (Reading Office) after the Second World War. Then it was used as an annexe to the University's St George's Hall from 1950 before being demolished in the 1960s.

After Park House was demolished, Whiteknights Hall was built in its place in 1963 - in 2009, most of this was also demolished and replaced with a new student hall called Mackinder Hall, named after the first Principal of the University College. The Park House estate extended up to a row of houses which were built near the eastern end of Upper Redlands Road, adjacent to the old boundary with the manor of Earley Whiteknights, by then known as Earley. This part of the estate was developed by the University to build additional student halls – Childs Hall and later Windsor Hall. There have been further developments here in the last decade.

Chapter 5

Housing Development of Central Whitley

Development of this part of Whitley started in earnest after the sale of the Whitley Park estate and the Cintra Lodge estate following the deaths of Samuel Palmer and Martin Hope Sutton respectively in 1903. This marked the end of the great land-owning period for Whitley that had lasted for several centuries since the Tudors.

Gradually, as the land of the Whitley Park estate was developed, several farms were demolished, starting with the Whitley Park Farm itself. Where Warwick Road was cut through and the adjoining Cintra Avenue was constructed in the Cintra Lodge estate, an avenue of pine trees was left from the Lodge estate and still exists along Cintra Avenue. Most of the Cintra Park estate remained intact as the Cintra Park Recreation Ground and continues as such to the present day, though the Cintra Lodge itself was demolished as part of Central Whitley development.

Warwick Road was to be the home of Edgar and Stanley Milward (of the Milwards shoe company) at a large house called 'Southview' which was close to the entrance of Cintra Park. Later, in the 1980s, a bungalow was added on part of the land, adjacent to the Park, for Edgar Milward to live and Southview was sold. Eventually the house and bungalow were both demolished and Milward Court, which has private flats for retired people, was erected in their place.

The previous photograph dated around 1910, shows Warwick Road as it was not long after it was developed though the road and footpaths are unmade but trees have been placed to line the sides of the road. At the far end is Cintra Park.

Along Shinfield Road and Marshall's Hill

Northcourt Avenue was the first major development of the Whitley Park Farm land. This was land sold off from Samuel Palmer's legacy in 1903 and covered the north-east part of the Whitley Park estate from the junction with Christchurch Road, running southwards behind houses along the west side of Shinfield Road, to Marshall's Hill. There it joined what was then Grosvenor Road (now Cressingham Road). The earliest developed houses were at the Christchurch Road end and building gradually worked southwards to Grosvenor Road. Northcourt Avenue was so called after Samuel Palmer's residence, Northcourt Lodge, in Hampstead, London. Most of its houses were developed around 1906 and in the 1930s, though some were erected later to in-fill.

St Patrick's Hall, designed by Charles Smith & Son (a company that was prominent in the town for many years), was built in 1913 on the site of the old Whitley Park Farm house and adjoining park land. The Hall was home to the No. 1 School of Aeronautics of the Royal Flying Corps during the Great War. On the west side of the Avenue, Nos. 12 to 22 were later purchased by the University for its use to build more residential halls. Apart from No. 20, which was demolished to allow greater access to St Patrick's Hall, the other houses remain along the front of and adjacent to the Hall. The main entrance to the 1990s-constructed Sherfield Hall and Student Village, which runs past No. 12 (Creighton Court), was opened up from Northcourt Avenue. In 2016, the University announced a proposal to demolish St Patrick's Hall and replace it with a more modern development of student accommodation in its place. The University Health Centre and Dental Surgery were opened in the early 1960s on previously undeveloped land in Northcourt Avenue at the Christchurch Road end.

Grosvenor Road was opened up on Marshall's Hill at the end of Northcourt Avenue around 1909/10 with four properties – Broomfield, Monks Barn, The Meadow and Marshall's Hill cottage. Later White Barn was added and then by

1926, there were another 23 houses as the Reading Council started its development of the Whitley estate. The housing along this road rapidly extended and by the end of that decade there were around 40 houses, together with the Tyndale Baptist Church, a Co-operative store and a Post Office, which were all located near the end of Northcourt Avenue. Staverton Road was also opened up as a northern offshoot of Grosvenor Road by the late 1920s. To save confusion, the name of Grosvenor Road was changed just after 1930 to Cressingham Road (there being a Grosvenor Road in Caversham). The new name referred to the large house, Cressingham, on the opposite side of Shinfield Road at the top of the hill.

Interestingly, the year after the Great War ended, a plan was put forward for a major housing development in the northern part of Central Whitley, from Home Farm down Northumberland Avenue to a point level with the World Turned Upside Down public house. The plan proposed a housing estate centred on the junction between Grosvenor Road, Long Barn Lane and Northumberland Avenue

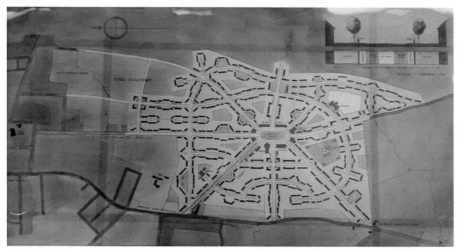

with radial roads spanning out from there. As can be seen from the plan above, it would have been like a village centre with major community facilities around it and housing distributed along the radial roads. It also proposed an extension of the town's tram service along Basingstoke Road and then through Long Barn Lane to the central village green. What it did not propose was a layout for a housing development beyond the area that it covered onward to Whitley Wood, so it was a bit short-sighted. Of course, we know the plan was not pursued but it is interesting that it was put forward and would certainly have created a different community from that which was developed over the following years.

The first large Council estate built by Reading Borough Council was the Shinfield Rise estate with tree names for the roads (Linden Road, Sycamore Road, etc.). This took place in 1919-20. A junction with Grosvenor Road was constructed when Sycamore Road was opened up to link across with Northcourt Avenue, parallel with the Shinfield Road. A school was not part of that initial development but soon became necessary with the influx of many children to the estate and so the Shinfield Road Council School (to become the Ridgeway School) was built in 1929 to save children having to travel to Redlands School or George Palmer School. The creation of this estate enabled the Council to provide homes for the expanding population of Reading town and for families to move into modern housing.

When the Shinfield Rise estate was being constructed, the builders used a horse and cart to transport materials around the site as can be seen in the photograph below, dated around 1924. Also in the background but not so easy to see is a steam traction engine. The houses in the distance are in Shinfield Road. It was obviously much harder work to build an estate of houses in those days than it is today.

The top of Northumberland Avenue

Building started down Northumberland Avenue from the top of the hill with the erection in 1909 of the Whitley Special School near to the top. Private properties were constructed nearby on both sides of the Avenue in that same year - houses at Nos. 18 and 20 and cottages at Nos. 1 and 3. By 1911, a total of some 60 private houses had been built down towards the bottom of the main slope of the hill – to the George Palmer School entrance on the west side and Newcastle Road on the east side.

In the photograph below, taken about 1910/11, the two houses on the right are Nos 18 (St Audries) and 20 (Ruardean) in Northumberland Avenue and to the left of them is the original 1909 Whitley Special School building. Further houses had been built down the first part of the hill but beyond that there was open land with the unmade road continuing down to the junction with Long Barn Lane.

After the Great War, house building down Northumberland Avenue resumed through the 1920s and 30s. A house by the corner of Newcastle Road became a dairy shop during the 1930s and it has seen many changes since, until recently it was a fishing-tackle shop.

To the south of Newcastle Road, 'The Northumberland Arms' public house was built in the 1930s, the land in that area having been used previously by the Reading Haulage Company. The part of the land next to the public house was later used by Smith's Coaches as the repair depot for their vehicles. That continued until the land was purchased for a row of shops, including a Bishop's supermarket, in the 1960s.

There were several more houses beyond the shops, leading to other land that had been farm land or, having been acquired by the Council, offered for allotments. This changed when the Southlands Secondary Girls' School was built and opened in 1960, though some allotments still remain between Newcastle Road and the Cintra Park.

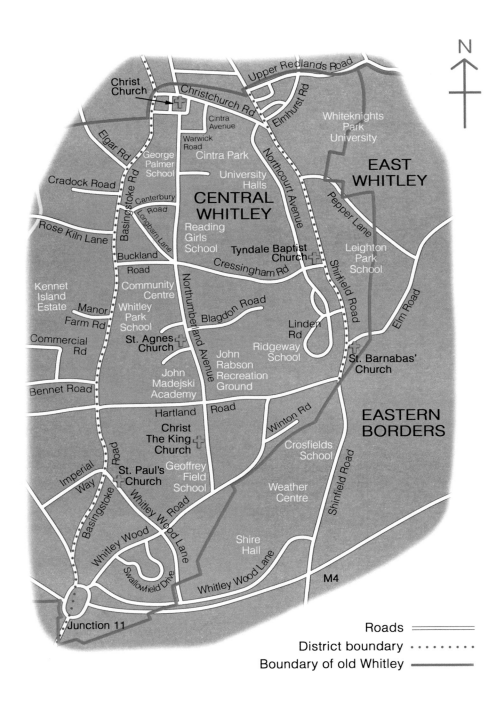

The map on the previous page shows the Central Whitley and East Whitley districts, largely as they are today and with the main roads and buildings named. East Whitley and the Eastern Borders are described in Chapter 7.

Many of the people who lived in this area will remember the sugar shortage in the 1970s. Mums with their children queued at the Bishop's store, sometimes as far as The Northumberland, at a certain time of the day when the manager would allow a restricted number of bags of sugar to be purchased by each of them.

The cottages at Nos. 1 and 3 remained the first properties at the top of the east side of Northumberland Avenue until the 1930s when three pairs of semi-detached houses were added at the top and all the numbering changed; 1 and 3 became 15 and 17 and all following houses had to change numbering accordingly.

In more recent times, plans were approved for removing two semi-detached houses (Nos 58 and 60) on the hill in Northumberland Avenue, near to George Palmer School, to open up a small estate utilising land at the rear and this was completed in 2008, the road being called 'Ella Garett Close'.

In place of the Avenue School, which was demolished in 2009, a new estate of houses was built, accessed from the Northumberland Avenue end. In addition, the construction was to include an extra-care housing scheme accessed from Basingstoke Road. The Care Home (Cedar Court), which was part-funded by a £3.1m housing grant, was completed in 2011 but there were structural problems with it and opening was delayed until late 2014. It comprised 40 flats over three floors accommodating 52 people, with wheel-chair access, beauty salon, café, meeting room and other facilities provided for the residents. The name given to the access road was 'Whitley Rise', referring to the Victorian property that preceded the Avenue School on the site. Meanwhile the private houses were completed in 2013 and quickly sold and the access road to them was named 'George Palmer Close' after the prominent Victorian local entrepreneur.

Middle Northumberland Avenue

Long Barn Lane, which had existed as a lane since the Middle Ages, was developed around 1930 - Tavistock Road and Yelverton Road were joined through to Buckland Road on the land where Ayres' Farm house had previously stood. The Long Barn Cottages still stood behind the Four Horseshoes Inn at that time, though they were later demolished and replaced with the existing motor vehicle workshops.

The Council had adopted the use of a series of names associated with the South West, e.g. Dawlish, Brixham, for the new roads developed in this area and beyond to the south, whereas names of more northern towns, e.g. Windermere, Ennerdale, had been used for many of the roads in the upper part of Central Whitley.

By the mid-1930s, Northumberland Avenue had been extended to the Honiton Road/Torrington Road roundabout. A parade of shops and the Whitley Heath Clinic were erected between Buckland Road and Honiton Road before the Second War. The South Reading Community Centre and a Youth Club were opened between the shops and the Health Clinic in the 1940s, replacing an earlier South Reading Community Association centre on the opposite side of the road.

The photograph above shows the official opening of the Whitley Maternity and Child Welfare Clinic in 1938. In the doorway are Alderman Arthur Clark and the Medical Officer of Health, Mr H J Milligan, and along the front are architect of the housing Department, Mr J S Paton, an unknown lady, Alderman Mrs Alice Jenkins, Mrs E E Langston and Councillor W. McIlroy.

Various facilities were established around the Cressingham Road/ Northumberland Avenue roundabout to meet the needs of the growing community in Central Whitley as the housing developments expanded further across this area. On one corner of Cressingham Road, Whitley Library opened on April 2nd 1935. The Library adapted itself in the early 21st century from being a place solely to read and/or borrow books to offer newer services to meet the needs of the community such as free internet access, study areas, toy library, in addition to books, CDs and DVDs. In 2016, a scheme was announced whereby Whitley Library would be moved into the South Reading Youth and Community Centre – nothing had happened by the end of that year but, in early 2017, it was announced that the Community Centre would be renovated to take the Library at a cost of around £0.75m but that would be offset by the sale of the old Library building, seen in the following photograph taken about 1980.

From the late 1940s, on the other corner of Cressingham Road and Northumberland Avenue was the Council's South Reading Building Maintenance depot, which was the base for the workmen who repaired and maintained the council houses on the Whitley estate. This was demolished in the 1960s, after much of the council housing in Whitley had been built and maintenance work was more centralised, and it was replaced with a block of flats (St Cecilia Court). Adjacent to the flats was a small pre-fab police office (Police Box 8) which was used as a base for the local Whitley policemen to report in, have meals and complete case reports – this existed from the late 1960s to the 1990s. Also there was a smaller Police Box with one desk in it at the end of Northumberland Avenue near Whitley Wood Road.

On the opposite corner of the roundabout at the junction of Buckland Road and Northumberland Avenue, the Berks and Reading Fire Brigade built a transport workshop where fire appliances were repaired and maintained. In the mid-1970s, it was demolished. In its place, the Carousel public house was erected, though that was also later demolished and replaced with flats (Carousel Court).

The photograph that follows was taken at the end of the Second World War and shows a motor bus travelling along Buckland Road towards Basingstoke Road junction, having just passed Brixham Road. In the distance, on the rising slope of the hill towards Shinfield Rise estate and the Ridgeway School at the top, can be seen what was known locally as the 'Cows hill'. The style of houses shown is typical of the many houses built for the Council at that time. It is understood that this photograph was taken from the roof of the old Savoy Cinema.

Lower end of Northumberland Avenue

Down Northumberland Avenue on the right-hand side just beyond the Hartland Road junction were three cottages which were probably originally farm cottages belonging to Goddard's Farm. Two were semi-detached and known as the

Eddystone cottages because, in the front garden, there was a lighthouse, which has been described as being about 5 to 6 feet tall. It was a landmark in the area and had a working lamp at the top. It was a replica of the real Eddystone Lighthouse, which stands on rocks on the south coast at the border between Cornwall and Devon. The third was Rose Farm Cottage. These were demolished to make way for for the proper surfacing of Northumberland Avenue and for the building of Christ the King Catholic Church in the 1950s.

During the 1930s up to the start of the Second World War, Northumberland Avenue had extended to include Blagdon Road, which was built up the side of the hill to join the Shinfield Rise estate. In Whitley Wood, Shirley Avenue and Woodside Way had been developed adjacent to Shinfield Park. Whitley Park School had been built in 1934 to serve the growing number of children in Lower Whitley, following the development of the Dawlish Road estate on the former Gray's Farm land down as far as Callington Road.

After the War and by 1950, the Avenue had extended to join Whitley Wood Road (albeit through a dirt track lane). Greenfields Road/Blandford Road estate to the west and the Foxhays Road estate to the east of the Avenue were being developed. With Hartland Road extended through to meet Whitley Wood Road in the east, the vast majority of today's Whitley road network had been constructed. Between Hartland Road and Blagdon Road, the John Rabson Recreation Ground was retained on the old farm land on the lower portion of the hill down to the Avenue, leaving the 'Cows Hill' on the slope up to the housing of the Shinfield Road estate and the Ridgeway School, both at the top of the hill.

The Second World War had quite an impact on the local community. On the roundabout at the junction of Northumberland Avenue and Hartland Road, an anti-aircraft gun was positioned that saw action when enemy aircraft, flying bombs, etc. passed over. This was manned from soldiers from the Army camp, which was located on the John Rabson Recreation Ground, and where Nissen huts had been erected to house them. It is understood that there may also have been a gun placement on the roundabout at the junction of Cressingham Road and Northumberland Avenue. Christ Church steeple was used as a look-out for air raids by the Home Guard. German prisoners-of-war were held at the RAF Camp at Shinfield Park until the end of the War.

Goddard's Farm, on the corner of Basingstoke Road and Hartland Road, was one of the last ones to be demolished on the main Whitley estate although there was still the Home Farm above Long Barn Lane (being run as a market garden by the

Selway family) and Whitley Wood Farm on the junction of Whitley Wood Lane and Basingstoke Road. During the 1950s, Goddard's Farm was replaced with the Ambrook Road development and some allotments while Home Farm was replaced with Canterbury Road and Home Farm Close. Playing fields were donated to the George Palmer Schools by the Selway family and the Long Barn Lane Children's Playground (later renamed Recreation Ground) was created for the use of the local community.

Around 2010, the Council embarked on a plan to brighten the green spaces around the town and, as part of this, planted hundreds of daffodils. The following photograph shows the island in the middle of Canterbury Road in glorious Spring colour in 2013.

St Agnes Church was built in 1939 between Callington Road and Stockton Road. The Ashmead Secondary Boys' School was constructed in 1951 between Stockton Road and Hartland Road, along Northumberland Avenue. On the opposite corner of the Hartland Road junction from the School, the Whitley Tavern public house was erected and, by the roundabout on the junction of Whitley Wood Lane and Whitley Wood Road, the Engineer's Arms public house was built – these two have since closed down and been replaced with flats.

As the final section of the Avenue was completed down to Whitley Wood Road, the Bourne Methodist Church was built in Exbourne Road in 1948, Geoffrey Field School in 1949 and Christ the King Catholic Church in 1959 with its school following in 1968. Up to this time, the Reading Corporation trolley-bus service terminated at a point about halfway between Hartland Road and Whitley Wood Road. Once the Avenue was completed, the terminus was moved to the end of Northumberland Avenue where it joins Whitley Wood Road. A parade of shops was opened in the Avenue opposite the new terminus.

Other developments in Central Whitley

Further estates of houses were built on the Whitley boundary along Whitley Wood Road - Wentworth Avenue and the Winton Road estate around 1950 and Alandale Close around 1960. To the south of Whitley Wood Road (actually in Shinfield parish at that time) was the RAF Training Camp and the associated Anson Crescent estate was developed around 1959/60 for the staff. A high chain link fence was erected around it. The fence was later taken down once the Camp had been closed.

One of the final pieces of the main Whitley estate to be developed was the Hexham Road estate between Newcastle Road and the Southlands Girls School in the 1960s. It included a Council-run residential nursing care home for the elderly called the Tanfield Centre. In 2010, it was announced that the Tanfield Centre was to be enhanced to handle many more dementia cases as a main Council facility for the town. This was completed and the Centre was re-opened in the autumn of 2011 as 'The Willows' Care Home'.

Other final developments were the former land of the old Whitley Wood Farm near the Basingstoke Road boundary of Whitley and the area to the east of Whitley Wood Lane. In the 1960s the Spencer Road estate was built on the farm land between Basingstoke Road and upper Whitley Wood Lane and then the Swallowfield Drive estate including the Whitley Wood Recreation Ground and a Lidl supermarket on Basingstoke Road. Beyond the Engineers Arms roundabout along lower Whitley Wood Lane, Margaret Close, Falmouth Road and beyond were opened up on the old Common land. Whitley Wood Lane was extended in the 1970s to form a link road from the Junction 11 of the M4 to the Shinfield Road. In 1992, Whitley Wood Fire Station was opened in Whitley Wood Road, close to the M4 Junction, to serve the south of the town, the major roads and a wider area as necessary.

The M4 provides a natural southern boundary to Reading, running west and east of Junction 11, even though the administrative boundary varied from it, particularly at Shinfield Park. So, once the M4 motorway around Reading was completed in 1971, this major highway was recognised as the southern boundary for the town under the 1972 Local Government Act.

Christchurch Gardens and the East side of Basingstoke Road

No. 12 Christchurch Gardens, on the corner of Northumberland Avenue, was used by the Abbey Junior School from 1928 to 1933 and was called 'Burge House'. It was then used until very recently as the lodging house for the Crown Court Judge (also known as the Red Judge) when appearing at Reading Crown Court as part of the circuit. Its use has more recently (in 2013) reverted to the Abbey Junior School and this time has been named The Abbey Gardens, after being much extended and renovated. A rear view of the house at No.12 is shown in the following photograph. This was taken shortly before the Abbey Junior School started its renovations.

No. 10 Christchurch Gardens was the home of the private 'No. IX' School from 1958 to 1978 under the ownership of Major Patrick Wormell, who ran the school as a preparatory school, including a nursery, for children up to 11 years of age. Before the Second War there had been a 'No IX' school at 'Sutherlands' house in Christchurch Road but it is not clear whether it had been run by the same family.

Nos. 4-10 Christchurch Gardens were demolished in the 1960s. In 1968, they were replaced with Christchurch Court, a sheltered housing/retirement home with 29 rooms, at Nos. 6-10 and with its warden's house at No.4.

At the beginning of the 1950s, going down the hill from Christchurch Gardens on the east side of Basingstoke Road, there were a row of houses down to Whitley Lodge, then the original Gillette factory that had just been opened at that time, then the Whitley Rise property, which was in use by the Reading Technical College in its early years, and then the George Palmer Schools. The Reading Technical College moved to King's Road in 1955.

By the early 1960s, Whitley Lodge and Whitley Rise had been demolished. The Avenue School had extended into the Whitley Rise land. Post Office Telephones, by 1960, had acquired the Whitley Lodge land and built the new Reading Trunk Exchange, which was officially opened in 1962 by Ernest Marples, the then Postmaster General. The Gillette factory next to Whitley Lodge had moved to a new large factory down Basingstoke Road on the west side near the World Turned Upside Down.

Post Office Telephones soon afterwards acquired the vacated Gillette factory land and also the houses in Basingstoke Road up to, and including, No.2 Christchurch Gardens in anticipation of major expansion over the coming years. It also acquired some houses in Northumberland Avenue. One of them was converted into a day nursery, called Bennet House after the then Telephone Manager of Reading Telephone Area. It was opened around 1970 for staff from the Trunk Exchange. It is now the privately run Northumberland Day Nursery. The planned expansion of the Trunk Exchange happened in a small way but much of the acquired land was not needed because of the development of much more compact higher-technology switching equipment, and so the houses in Northumberland Avenue were sold privately in the 1980s. Also sold was the old Gillette land, which was then used for building the small Avenue Heights estate.

The photograph at the foot of the previous page, taken in 2016, is of the BT Trunk Exchange from Basingstoke Road.

The George Palmer School, the first school on the Whitley Park estate, was built in 1907 in Basingstoke Road next door to Whitley Rise. When the school buildings were demolished in 2004 and replaced with a new building in a slightly different location, the land fronting Basingstoke Road was cleared and used for the construction of a block of apartments called Scholar's Place that was opened in 2007.

In 1988, major road resurfacing took place in Basingstoke Road and the following photograph was taken after a water main was damaged. In the distance can be seen a Reading Bus about to turn into Christchurch Gardens, which was the diversion route for the Whitley Wood buses for the duration of the road works.

Below the George Palmer Schools was the estate that comprised Surrey, Winchester and Lincoln Roads. This was opposite the start of Elgar Road. The Home Farm estate was below those houses leading down to the Four Horseshoes Inn.

Also in Basingstoke Road was the famous Nicholl's Sauce and Pickle Works (owned by Walter Nicholl) next door to the Savoy Cinema near the northern corner of Buckland Road. On this northern corner of Buckland Road was the Reading Co-operative Stores and there were several other shops opened up on the southern corner and also into Buckland Road. Both the Pickle factory and the

Savoy had been demolished by 1961 and they were replaced with a 'Fine Fare' supermarket. Later, in the 1980s, that supermarket was replaced with a golf shop, which has since changed to an outdoor clothing and equipment store.

Housing continued to be built along the east side of Basingstoke Road and this extended down to Goddard's Farm in 1950. There was a section from Hartland Road where allotments are today and, beyond that, further housing was added near to the Whitley Wood Garage and the shops on the corner of Whitley Wood Lane by St Paul's Church.

Shinfield Road

On the corner of Shinfield Road and Northcourt Avenue was an old building that had been used formerly as St George's Hostel by Reading University and then, from 1947, for the St Joseph's Convent Junior School, which moved to Lydford Road behind the secondary St Joseph's Convent School in 1988. This old building was demolished shortly afterwards and, in 1990, Marlborough House, an apartment block for older people, was opened. Most of the west side of Shinfield Road had been developed for housing by 1950 as far as the junction with Whitley Wood Road. The 'Merry Maidens' public house had been open since the mid-19th century and was rebuilt before the Second World War. There were a number of shops opened on the corner of Whitley Wood Road and Shinfield Road.

These final pieces of development of the Central Whitley estate completed the replacement of the main part of the farmland that had been left a hundred years previously in the Samuel Palmer and Martin Hope Sutton legacies.

Chapter 6

Industrial & Commercial Development of West Whitley

In the census returns of the 19th century, the area to the west of the Basingstoke Road from Milman Road down to Hartley Court Road was described as West Whitley. (For the purposes of this section, that description covers the area from Elgar Road southwards, the rest being covered in the 'Development after the 1887 Boundary Changes up to the turn of the century' section of Chapter 3).

Until the 1950s, this area was largely undeveloped, being predominantly farmland (with the associated farmhouses and cottages) and meadow land or flood plains for the River Kennet and the Foudry Brook as they meandered in from the west of Reading and from the south of Reading respectively. The farms were Smallmead Farm, Little Lea Farm and Whitley Manor Farm (with Hartley Court Farm, Great Lea Farm and Church Lane Farm, all in Shinfield, being just outside the bounds of Whitley). On Basingstoke Road, opposite the Four Horseshoes Inn, was a small number of terraced houses (the six houses of Rhinefield Terrace and the thirteen houses of Ashley Terrace) and further down at Whitley Wood was the Grenadier public house.

The only industrial works in the first half of the 20th century were the Whitley Kiln, closed down in the 1950s, and the Corporation's Sewage Works on the Kennet by Manor Farm. On Manor Farm land during the early 1920s, there was a Smallpox Camp sited for isolation purposes and this became the Corporation Isolation Hospital out in the open area behind the Grenadier towards the Foudry Brook and Smallmead Farm. This Isolation Hospital was finally closed in 1959. The rest was open fields which were, like much of Whitley at that time, a pleasure to wander past and through. However, that was all to change very quickly.

The Elgar Road section of the Whitley Kiln estate, to the east of the Co-operative Printing Works and WW Hall builders' merchants in Katesgrove, was to become the site of the commercial operation of Clarks builders' merchants, which later became Graham Clark. After a fire destroyed the warehouses, that business moved to Rose Kiln Lane Industrial Estate and the land was taken over by a branch of Keyline which still operates there. Meanwhile a 3 acre site on the old Whitley Kiln land was bought by Gowrings Ford dealership in 1963. Cradock Road was cut through to the old Rose Kiln land and, via Boulton Road, linked with Rose

Kiln Lane. This whole area was developed for light industrial use from the 1950s onwards.

Also to the west of Basingstoke Road, between the Gillette factory and the Whitley Wood Lane junction, both Bennet Road (together with Commercial Road running to the rear of Gillette's factory) and Acre Road were opened up after the Second World War. This area was developed as industrial/commercial estates. Bennet Road became the home for the Reading Corporation Transport Depot as well as other vehicle centres and Acre Road became the home to various manufacturing and distribution companies.

The map that follows shows the modern shape of West Whitley. This includes the waterways (River Kennet and Foudry Brook) together with the western Whitley boundary, the old northern boundary with Reading and the main roads and buildings.

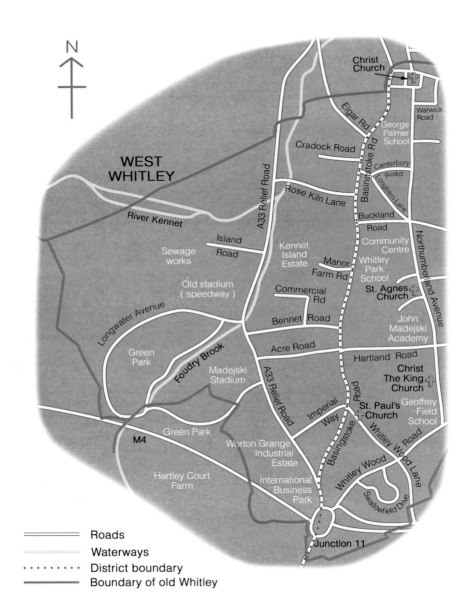

N

WEST
WHITLEY

Christ
Church

Warwick
Road

Elgar Rd

George
Palmer
School

Cradock Road

Canterbury
Road

Basingstoke Rd

Longbarn Lane

Rose Kiln Lane

A33 Relief Road

River Kennet

Buckland
Road

Island
Road

Community
Centre

Sewage
works

Kennet
Island
Estate

Whitley
Park
School

Northumberland Avenue

Manor
Farm Rd

Old stadium
(speedway)

St. Agnes
Church

Commercial
Rd

John
Madejski
Academy

Longwater Avenue

Bennet Road

Acre Road

Hartland Road

Christ
The King
Church

Green
Park

Foudry Brook

Madejski
Stadium

A33 Relief Road

Imperial
Way

St. Paul's
Church

Geoffrey
Field
School

Green Park

Basingstoke Road

Whitley Wood Road

M4

Worton Grange
Industrial
Estate

Whitley Wood Lane

Hartley Court
Farm

International
Business
Park

Whitley Wood

Swallowfield Drive

Junction 11

===== Roads
===== Waterways
·········· District boundary
——— Boundary of old Whitley

Once the A33 Relief Road was constructed and linked with the far end of Rose Kiln Lane, this route offered easy access to the town and to the M4 as well as further afield so it became much more attractive to businesses. A Makro cash-and-carry supplier was built between Cradock Road and Elgar Road. On the south side of Rose Kiln Lane, the Brunel Retail Park was constructed with businesses such as Laura Ashley occupying units on the site. Safeway had built a supermarket on the corner of Rose Kiln Lane and Basingstoke Road in the 1980s, replacing Reading Garage which had been on that site since the 1960s. This supermarket was later taken over by Morrison's. Next down Basingstoke Road is a multi-unit site that was opened in 2015/16 and includes an Aldi store. Beyond that is the site first occupied in the 1960s by B & Q, the DIY store. That store later moved to the Reading Gate Retail Park on the A33 Relief Road and the site was taken over by BJ's Luxury Bingo. Between the Bingo building and Manor Farm Road, Thames Water established its Reading operations centre, later moving to a site by the River Thames at Reading Bridge. Beyond Manor Farm Road was the Gillette factory, opened in the 1950s, together with the Hansen laboratories.

Brick and Tile Works

Brick making was one of the major industries in Reading, with the Katesgrove and Waterloo Kilns forming the largest sources of bricks in the south of Reading. However, the Rose Kiln and later the Whitley Kiln were also significant producers. Building the kilns close to the river was as important as needing to be close to a good source of clay. The bricks from these kilns were used in large quantities around Reading and also the surrounding area, with many coloured varieties being produced and used in pattern.

Whitley Kiln was developed around 1900 by Samuel H Gwilliam on land across the corner of Basingstoke Road and Elgar Road and extending back to the river Kennet and down through what is now Cradock Road to Rhinefield Terrace on Basingstoke Road. The company was called Gwilliam and Sons Steam Brickworks. Mr Gwilliam himself lived in a house called 'North View' near the corner of Elgar Road and later in 'The Poplars' in the same area – he died in 1951 aged 89. The business was owned by the Gwilliam family for many years and was closed during the 1950s, by which time some of the Whitley Kiln land had been occupied by Wilkins civil engineering contractors and Cowley contractors.

Rose Kiln was opened up as a brick and tile works, just a bit further south from where Whitley Kiln was to be established, along the side of the river Kennet opposite Fobney Meadow. It was shown in the 1851 census (though not in any other census) with John Wood being the brick maker and was still shown on the local map around 1880 as being in existence. The 1861 census does show a Rose Farm near to where the Kiln was located so there may have been a link there. However the Kiln did not survive for long and by 1900 it had been closed. The lane which led to it from Basingstoke Road was much longer lasting and was later called Rose Kiln Lane as it is today (though it has been much extended across the river to form part of the modern A33 Relief Road with a Rose Kiln industrial and business estate at the Coley end).

Some of the businesses that emerged in West Whitley

The **_Gowrings Ltd Ford dealership_** was built on the corner of Basingstoke Road and Elgar Road in 1963 on a three acre site that was formerly part of the Whitley Kiln site. It replaced the Service Station that had been there since the 1920s, adjacent to the Whitley Kiln frontage and office. In later years, the dealership changed hands from Gowrings to other Ford agents (Reg Vardy and Jack Davis). Recently it returned into the hands of Gowrings Ltd and part of the site was then shared with a Peugeot dealership. However, in 2016, the Gowrings dealership was closed down then, shortly afterwards, the Peugeot dealership also closed leaving the whole site vacant.

Gillette UK Ltd started on Whitley Hill just after the Second World War in about 1948. However it had moved on by the late 1950s to its present location in Basingstoke Road nearly opposite the World Turned Upside Down public house. This photograph shows the factory as it was in 1962.

Little Miss Muffett Junket, produced at the **_Hansen Laboratories_,** moved from London Street (after beginning production in 1916 in Queen's Road) to a factory next to Gillette in the late 1950s. This factory continued in production beyond the company's 75th anniversary in the 1990s. A little further south was the **_Warwick Brothers_** timber merchants, which had been at the location since the 1930s. Those have both now gone and the land south of Gillette's factory on the corner of Bennet Road is occupied by Jewson builders' merchants. In the meantime, Gillette UK Ltd was taken over by Proctor and Gamble, though still trading under the same name.

In Cradock Road, a new plant was built by the Welsh linen hire company, **_Afonwen Laundry_,** to service a number of hotels in London and the South East. It cost £4m and opened in 2013 with more than 100 jobs offered. In 2015, a separate second laundry facility and costing £4m was opened next to the first with another 60 jobs on offer.

Smallmead Farm land, within the boundary of Whitley, was used for the Reading Speedway and Greyhound Stadium and also the civic amenity from the 1970s. Later the Stadium was closed down and the civic amenity moved to Island Road next door to the new Sewage Works. The former site of the civic amenity at Smallmead was developed for the Madejski Stadium and Hotel complex which opened in 1998.

Digital Electronics Corporation opened its offices in Basingstoke Road, just beyond the Post House Hotel opposite the Whitley Wood Lane junction, in the 1970s and later moved to occupy the vacant former County Council building at Shire Hall. The company closed its operation in Reading in 1998 after it had been taken over by Compaq which itself was bought by Hewlett Packard in 2002.

Foster-Wheeler Energy Ltd has its largest operation in the UK at Shire Hall in Shinfield Park to which it moved in the late 1990s from the old Vincent's car showroom site by Reading station.

Horseman Coaches Ltd is based at 2 Acre Road. In 1977 Keith Horseman started a small Reading-based coach operation. Then in 1984, with a rapidly growing business, he acquired the familiar Reading coach company, Smith's Coaches. Now Horseman's runs more than 100 coaches focussing mainly on school transport and coach hire.

Robert Darvall started a removal business in Acre Road in 1926 from a warehouse there. From 1960, Ken Darvall took over as MD of the business and in

1989 a new warehouse at 4 Acre Road was opened to allow further expansion of the firm.

The Sewage Farm and the 'Whitley Whiff'

The local Reading Borough Council acquired land outside the then borough to set up a sewage farm to serve the town. Manor Farm in Whitley was purchased and a major project set in train. In 1875, the Reading Corporation Waste Water Treatment Works was constructed at the Farm and opened at Fobney lock. The site continued to be used, with upgrades, for the treatment of sewage and waste water until the end of the 20th century, by which time the Works had been taken over into private ownership and was run by Thames Water. Many improvements had been made up to 1963. Land nearby was also acquired to open up a new drainage scheme and this was opened in 1881. These two much improved treatment facilities at Manor Farm heralded a great improvement in sanitation and health for the town of Reading and the Whitley Manor itself.

However, by the 1980s, the growth of the town, the increased population and the increasing effects on the local community of the renowned 'Whitley Whiff' meant that the old 19th century plant could no longer be improved to meet the future demands on it. The Whitley Whiff was a result of the sewage processing at the Thames Water Authority's works and, depending on the direction of the wind, it polluted the air over Whitley (the prevailing wind being from the west, of course) and reached up and over Whitley Street and across Katesgrove and even into the edges of the town when the wind came from the south-west. Around 1990, Thames Water started making an attempt to eliminate the Whiff and spent some £3.5m and then a further £4.9m up to 1995 but this was not enough to make a lasting difference.

It was finally decided that a new modern processing plant was required on a new site. A location in Island Road was identified, not far from the Manor Farm site. This Island Road site was owned by the Reading Borough Council and had been used as a waste location including old sewage sludge and had to be cleared before the new treatment works could be built. Clearance work started in 2001 while design of the new facility was under way. A project team, involving Thames Water, was commissioned to carry out the design through to completion of the work which included renovation of the separate Reading sewage pumping station.

The new site was put into operation in March 2004 at a cost of £80m. The development was six years in the design, comprising four 60ft high egg-shaped aluminium digesters, an interesting sight which can be seen from the Household Waste Recycling Centre next door. Transfer of sewage management from Manor Farm was completed later that year, with the capacity to serve 284,000 consumers. It was officially opened in January 2005 and was one of the most advanced treatment works in the UK. After it had opened, the local population was 'holding its breath' to see how successfully it worked!

Reading Gate Retail Park

One of the early constructions along the A33 Relief Road was this Retail Park with its main occupant being B&Q, which moved from its Basingstoke Road site, and several other occupants including Carpetright, Currys PC World and TK Maxx.

Madejski Stadium Complex

In addition to the Madejski Stadium (see the 'Recreation and Entertainment' chapter), John Madejski funded the construction of a hotel as part of the complex, the Millennium Madejski hotel. John Madejski also established a local radio station (107 FM) at the Madejski stadium site in 2001, competing with Radio 210 (2-ten) and Radio Berkshire as local radio stations. The station name was later changed to 107 Jack FM. In 2016, the new Thai owners of the Stadium complex applied for planning approval for a new development called Royal Elm Park. It would include some 600 homes, a new hotel, an ice rink and a Convention Centre together with a multi-storey car park and various retail outlets.

This photograph, taken in 2010, shows the entrance to the Stadium to the left and the Millennium Madejski Hotel on the right.

Reading International Business Park

To meet the continuing growth in demand for commercial property and facilities, expansion continued unabated along the A33 Relief Road and surrounding area. Following behind the Worton Grange 'Berkshire Brewery' that had opened in 1980 and which was owned by Scottish and Newcastle Breweries, the Reading International Business Park was opened in 2000, offering capacity for several thousand jobs. It was initially occupied by Worldcom, a major American telecommunications company that had started operating in the UK. Worldcom (later becoming MCI after being taken over by that company) was replaced by the American communications company, Verizon, on the same site in 2006. The original International Business Park building was constructed between Worton Grange and the A33 Relief Road as a single crescent-shaped building with six wings at the rear; the site includes the old Little Lea farmhouse. A later addition was the Reading 360 circular office building which completed the Park.

Green Park

The Green Park development was started in 1997 by PRUPIM (a property development business owned by the Prudential). It was designed as a 195-acre environmentally-friendly business park close to the M4 and a striking design feature was an 11-acre lake, a kilometre long, winding through the middle. The site was expected to provide office space for more than 7000 employees. A number of leading IT companies, such as Cisco and Logica, soon took up space and the Park has since erected its own wind turbine together with signage masts which are all visible for quite a distance away. The 120m wind turbine – a first for Reading area and given much publicity locally – had been designed by Norman Foster for Prudential and Ecotricity and was brought into use in 2005/6 to bring *'clean, wind-generated electricity to Reading'*, generating 3.5m kWh of electricity per year, enough to power 1500 homes.

Green Park continued to fill with additional companies moving into the new eco-friendly buildings, including Thames Water and HSBC, creating employment opportunities for many people who may have been affected by the recession of 2009. The management company also provided recreational facilities including an all-weather pitch and running tracks, together with a large conference centre, nursery, restaurant and café. In 2007, plans were agreed with the Council to develop a mini-town in Green Park (some 700+ houses, flats, care units for elderly, together with community facilities) and also a railway station. The plans were re-approved in 2010 to allow a longer period to complete the whole development. In 2011, the whole enterprise was sold by Prudential to Oxford Properties, a Canadian business.

In 2012, Huawei – a major Chinese telecommunications company – moved its headquarters from Basingstoke to Green Park. The new £12m railway station serving the Green Park/Madejski Stadium area was confirmed in late 2014 when an investment of £6.4m by the Berkshire Local Transport Body was announced. The work was to start in 2016 and be finished in 2017. The station would be a halt on the Reading-Basingstoke line and sited near the Green Park's main road, Longwater Avenue. The rest of the £12m would come from the Council, the owners and private investment. By 2017, the work had still not started but additional funding had been provided for the station construction, making £16.3m in total. The completion date was put back to 2019.

Berkeley Group was given the planning approval in late 2015 to proceed with a mixed-use development including 657 homes under the name of Green Park Village. There were some 6000 people working in the Park in 2015 with at least 50 global companies occupying the site.

Worton Grange Industrial Park

Scottish Courage, the owner of the Berkshire Brewery at Worton Grange, became S&N UK and in 2003 bought the HP Bulmer group. In 2008, closure of the Reading brewery was proposed, followed shortly after by the purchase of the S&N UK business by Heineken NV. The Berkshire Brewery, however, was given its 'last orders' and closed down completely in March 2010. This then completed the demise of the last of the famous Reading '3 Bs', Beer joining the Bulbs and Biscuits in leaving the town. The brewery was dismantled over the following months and then, in the autumn of 2011, the Reading Borough Council and Wokingham Borough Council approved proposals from Tesco to build a distribution centre on the site. The £27m Tesco centre would create some 1000 jobs and would comprise a 60ft high warehouse and a vehicle maintenance depot with office space and large parking area for staff and over 200 lorries. It was assessed that there would be no more vehicle movement from the site than had been the case with the brewery. Construction of the distribution centre that covers nearly 1m sq. ft., started in January 2012 and was completed and opened in mid-2013, creating one of the largest warehouses in Europe.

Hewlett Packard closed its offices at Worton Grange Industrial Park in October 2006, after 18 years at the site, and the last of 1200 staff moved from its Worton Grange HQ to its refurbished building at Amen Corner in Bracknell. In 2012, the vacant 20.5 acre site between Imperial Way and Basingstoke Road was earmarked by Worton Grange Industrial Limited for a new housing estate of 300 homes, a supermarket and other stores and a public consultation began. The site was purchased by a development company in 2014 and plans were being prepared for submission to the Council for a scheme including 250 homes, a new hotel and retail space under the commercial name of Reading Gateway. In 2016, local development group Kier Property were given the planning approval to build 175 homes on the Imperial Way site together with commercial units, a hotel and various other buildings. It was later confirmed that there would be a 120-bed Premier Inn hotel with a Beefeater Restaurant and a Costa Coffee drive-through as part of the £75m development.

Kennet Island Estate

In the middle of the West Whitley commercial area, situated around the Manor Farm Road between Bennet Road and Rose Kiln Lane and between the rear of the Gillette factory and the Foudry Brook, a new housing development was started in 2006. This was named the 'Kennet Island' estate, with the initial phase of housing completed in 2007. Nearly 1400 homes were built by the developers, St James Group, in the total scheme. Primary access was from the A33 Relief Road, passing over the Brook, though it can also be accessed from Commercial Road. These homes were a mix of apartments and houses with tower blocks ranging from three to eight storeys and two-storey family houses. Parking spaces were concealed under raised podiums with community facilities on top. In 2014, a further phase of development of apartments was launched – Skylark House – by the developers. Plans for the final phase of the scheme were approved by the Reading Council in mid-2013, permitting the building of 444 apartments and 102 houses.

At the entrance to the Kennet Island estate, adjacent to the A33 Relief Road, another hotel development was the opening of a Hilton Hotel in May 2009. This was built to be both close to the M4 junction 11 and the Madejski Stadium and also within easy reach of the town centre thus offering further hotel accommodation at the heart of the burgeoning commercial district in the south of Reading. Very close to the Hotel, a new independent 50-bedroom hospital (CircleReading) was constructed and opened in the summer of 2012. The hospital cost £50m and was designed to provide surgery and outpatient service for NHS and private patients.

Chapter 7

East Whitley and the Eastern Borders:
Upper Redlands Road to Shinfield Park and the M4

This chapter describes the border area which historically lay across the boundary between Whitley and either Earley Whiteknights (northern part) or Shinfield (southern part). It covers the area that today reaches from Upper Redlands Road via Whiteknights Park, Leighton Park School (formerly Pepper Manor and which includes that part previously the separate Cressingham Park). It also covers the eastern borders of what has loosely been called Shinfield Park, as far as the M4 boundary to the south of Whitley Wood. This is all a significant area of former park land, along the eastern and south-eastern boundary of the old Whitley Manor. It was mainly developed during the expansion which followed the opening of the Great Western Railway at Reading in 1840 that had encouraged many aspiring and wealthy families to set up home on the outskirts of the town.

In the mid-18th century, Upper Redlands Road did not exist except as a field boundary (probably within Red Lane Farm). Whiteknights Park was smaller (at that time not extending to Shinfield Road - which was then called Shinfield Lane - but ending roughly along the Earley Whiteknights boundary with Whitley). Leighton Park was farm land, belonging to what was then the Pepper Farm, and there was a house on Cressingham Park which may have been the original large house there. The boundary between Whitley and Earley Whiteknights ran through the eastern side of Leighton Park and Cressingham Park. Beyond that to the south was common land, leading to the junction of what is now Elm Road with Shinfield Road. Elm Road was the boundary between Earley to the north and Shinfield to the south. Further south was the Shinfield Green which was common land until the Enclosure Act of 1855, after which it was bought by Sir Alexander Cobham, the then owner of Pepper Manor and Shinfield Park. To the west ran a lane through Whitley Wood Common and then along the southern boundary of Whitley - that lane became what is now Whitley Wood Road.

Modern East Whitley and Eastern Borders are shown on the map on page 52. East Whitley has a boundary with Earley and just touches the boundary with Shinfield. The Eastern Borders are all within Shinfield. The extent of this whole area includes the University of Reading campus at Whiteknights Park through to the former Shire Hall building and the M4.

The following photograph shows the original Whiteknights House, now known as 'old Whiteknights House' - a rear view of the building with the small surrounding gardens. At the time of John Heelas (see Chapter 4), there was a large conservatory across part of the rear of the house.

On the brow of the hill (then known as 'Nores Hill'), in Shinfield Park, was an old property called 'Goodrest'. There was also 'The Grove', an 18th century property, and 'Shinfield Lodge', which was built between 'Goodrest' and 'The Grove'. Little had changed by the end of the 18th century, except that Whiteknights Park had expanded west over the Earley boundary to the Shinfield Road, while under the ownership of the Marquis of Blandford, and it was more like its size today.

During the 19th century, 'Pepper Manor' was built on the Pepper Farm estate (later to be known as Leighton Park) and Pepper Lane was cut through from Shinfield Road to Elm Road. Pepper Manor was given to Captain Alexander Cobham as a wedding present in 1863. In 1886 the Manor was put up for sale as Leighton Park and then acquired by Quakers for the establishment of Leighton Park School in 1889.

Two large houses were built along the south side of Pepper Lane abutting Leighton Park - Shrublands and Trelawney – just outside the Whitley boundary. The part of Southern Hill that later became Upper Redlands Road was opened up at the north of Whiteknights Park. This Park was developed after the Marquis of Blandford was forced to sell (through financial difficulties) and it then moved into the hands of the Goldsmid family in the mid-19th century. Cressingham Park was developed and properties were built on the southern junction of Shinfield Road and Elm Road in the area where 'The Sportsman' public house now stands.

Crossing Southern Hill and running through to the Redlands Road junction with Shinfield Road was Alexandra Road. This road had been named in honour of Edward VII's wife, Alexandra of Denmark (hence Denmark Road nearby). At the junction of Southern Hill with Alexandra Road, a villa was built for George Palmer and it was apparently originally called 'Upper Redlands' (according to contemporary directories) but later renamed as 'Elmhurst' when his son, George William Palmer, took over the house and extended it.

Around 1900, the name 'Upper Redlands' was given to the adjacent section of Southern Hill that led from Redlands Road to Eastern Avenue, becoming Upper Redlands Road, and the name 'Elmhurst' was given to the part of Alexandra Road that led from Upper Redlands Road to Shinfield Road, thus becoming Elmhurst Road (though retaining its original Alexandra Road numbering).

In the 1850s, a road was opened up leading from Redlands Road through to Upper Redlands Road via a dog-leg turn. This became known as New Road and it contains a number of old and interesting cottages. Later, towards the end of the century, another road was cut through from Redlands Road to Elmhurst Road and named Marlborough Avenue, reminiscent of the Marquis of Blandford, the former owner of Whiteknights Park who became the Duke of Marlborough.

On the corner of Elmhurst Road and Upper Redlands Road, on the opposite side to Elmhurst House, there is a small piece of land with a hexagonal building in the centre and some other buildings around it. This was originally part of the Elmhurst estate and, around the turn of the 19th century, was known as Elmhurst Park. It contained stables for the horses and coaches for the main house. Around 1925, as motor cars had taken over from coach and horses, a dairy run by Frank Pym was established on the land and he used this as a depot from which to deliver milk by horse and cart to the locality from then until 1942. This dairy was called the Elmhurst Farm Dairy and Harry Pidgeon took over from Frank Pym and continued to run it until the 1970s.

Then it was used by the Museum of English Rural Life as a store for some of its large farm vehicles. Most recently it has been replaced with a small group of residential properties instead of the stables, though the hexagonal building (now 11 Elmhurst Road) still stands in the middle and that has been listed.

This is a recent photograph of the building taken from inside Whiteknights Park.

Surrounding Elmhurst Park and along Elmhurst Road towards Shinfield Road was a larger 12-acre piece of land which was leased to the University College by George W Palmer in 1909 for use as an Athletics Ground and bequeathed to the College in 1913 on his death. This use continued until the entire estate was acquired by the University and still forms part of the sports area to this day.

In Upper Redlands Road, between Elmhurst Road and New Road, two houses at Nos. 35 and 35A were acquired by the University and used for the Department of Music. The use of these has now changed since the Music Department was closed a few years ago.

In 1947, the freehold of Whiteknights Park and its six composite leased estates (including Whiteknights House and Blandford Lodge), together with the separately leased Park House, were acquired by the University of Reading.

The three properties in Shinfield (Goodrest, The Grove and Shinfield Lodge) on Nores Hill had been requisitioned by the RAF to establish a training camp and convalescent home during the Second World War. Nores Hill was the highest point available for this purpose with an extensive view and range across the Kennet Valley. 'The Grove' was used by the WRAF. 'Shinfield Lodge', by then part of Leighton Park Junior School's estate, was requisitioned by the RAF Flying Training Command as its Headquarters in 1940 and continued to stay there until 1968. After the War, Crosfields School was established at 'Goodrest' while the Meteorological Office set up a training college nearby. The RAF camp continued through to the 1970s - during which time an estate of houses had been built for their use on the land down the hill to Whitley Wood Road – and, after that time, the residual property was returned for civilian use. In 2013, a memorial plaque was unveiled in the grounds of 'Shinfield Lodge' as a tribute to the brave RAF crews who died for their country.

Meanwhile the Whitley part of the Nores Hill land had been taken over for development and the housing estate encompassing Winton Road and Egerton Road was built.

In 1974, Reading changed from a County Borough to a District within the County of Berkshire under local government changes at that time. Much of the responsibilities previously held by the Borough were transferred to Berkshire County Council, including Police, Water, Fire and the Regional Hospital Board. In 1980, a new Shire Hall was built on the land where The Grove had been demolished in Shinfield Park, close to the M4 and highly visible for some distance around, replacing the old Shire Hall in The Forbury in the town centre. It was decided in 1995 to abolish the Berkshire County Council and replace it with six Districts. The new Shire Hall was then redundant and was taken over by Digital and then later by Foster-Wheeler, which is the current occupant.

The European Centre for Medium-range Weather Forecasts (ECMWF) was established between Crosfields and the Meteorological Office Training College in the mid-1970s.

In the second half of the 20th century, the eastern part of the Shinfield Road/ Pepper Lane/Elm Road triangle, where the large houses 'Shrublands' and 'Trelawney' had stood, were cleared and new houses were built in the Harcourt Drive estate. Another estate was opened up at the bottom end of that triangle adjacent to 'The Sportsman,' which was a 19th century public house. Finally Devonshire Park was built on part of the old Cressingham Park estate, land that Leighton Park School had sold for development.

St Barnabas Church was built in 1925 near the corner of Elm Road with Shinfield Road and then shops and a garage were erected along the Shinfield Green frontage.

Significant properties in this area

Elmhurst

This house was built in 1862 as a villa style property, designed by Joseph Morris for George Palmer, on land adjacent to Whiteknights Park along Southern Hill. The estate also included extensive land on the opposite side of Southern Hill that was later sold and developed as Avebury Square and other properties. A photograph of George Palmer in his later years is shown here.

Above the entrance door to Elmhurst House there is a keystone in the arch with the inscription of George Palmer's initials 'GP'. At the time that the house was built, it appears to have been called 'Upper Redlands'. After George Palmer moved to The Acacias in London Road in 1865, the house 'Upper Redlands' was renamed 'Darlinghurst' by its lessor, J Dyke. It then became 'Elmhurst House' when George William Palmer (son of George Palmer) took it over around 1878. He continued to live there during the next 20 years until he moved out around 1900 to Marlston House near Newbury which had been the country estate of his (by then) late father. Elmhurst was then leased to Herbert Pretty (a University Board member) until 1935 and then acquired by M Audley Fouquet Sutton (of the Sutton's Seeds family) before being purchased by the University in 1939.

During George William Palmer's ownership of Elmhurst, it was extended at both ends to provide large reception rooms and extra servants' quarters. After the University acquired the house and estate, it was extended further to convert it into student accommodation under the name of St George's Hall. More recently, additional modern student accommodation has been built in a separate building in the grounds.

Goodrest Estate

This estate once belonged to the Englefield family. In 1630, a large house was brick-built for Sir Francis Englefield and was called Shinfield Park. It is reputed that King Charles I stayed there (presumably at the time of the Siege of Reading during the Civil War) and said that he had had 'a goode reste' while the guest of Sir Francis and thus the name was adopted from that time. During the late 18th/ early 19th century, the old house was demolished and a new 'Goodrest' built in its place for Edward Willes Esq. around 1820. This house, described as built in the *ornamental Gothic style*, was later sold by his son, William, to a Mr John Dawson Mayne according to the 'Victoria County History of Berkshire'. The property straddled the boundary between Whitley and Shinfield. During the Second World War the estate became part of the RAF Training Command HQ and then in 1946 was bought by Leighton Park School as its Junior School, after the War being renamed Crosfields School.

Some features of the Eastern Borders

European Centre for Medium-Range Weather Forecasts (ECMWF)

This high security centre opened in 1975 and is an internationally renowned and world-leading meteorological centre, employing more than 220 people from across Europe. It provides medium-range forecasts (day 3 to day 14) and also long-range forecasts (beyond 14 days) for initially 18 and now 28 member countries in Europe. The centre takes information from satellite systems and predicts hurricanes, droughts and base information for constructing shipping forecasts. The exact forecasts produced are used by the Food and Agriculture Organisation and global organisations for harvest, drought and malaria prediction as well as by transport systems (shipping, air) across Europe. The national Meteorological Offices develop short range forecasts (one to two day, as seen on television).

When opened in 1975, it began working closely with the other meteorological centres close by – the Department of Meteorology at the University, the Meteorological Office in Bracknell and the Training College next door at Shinfield (since relocated to Bracknell) – this formed an excellent concentration of expertise (Reading is also the home of the Royal Meteorological Society). As the global environment becomes a more and more prominent feature in coming years, because of climate change concerns, the ECMWF will serve as a most important supplier to the European Commission and other global political and environmental interests.

Meteorological Office

The Meteorological Office in Bracknell opened its College in 1936 and moved it to Shinfield Park in 1971 after the RAF had vacated the site. The Training College provided forecasts for trans-Atlantic flights then more recently focussed on training overseas operatives in the skills required to use and analyse computerised systems for forecasting weather. The College was closed at this site and returned to Bracknell as part of the preparation for development of Shinfield Park in the first decade of the 21st century.

Shire Hall/Digital/Foster Wheeler

The new Shire Hall was built on the Shinfield Park estate in the 1970s to replace the previous home of Berkshire County Council in The Forbury in Reading town centre. In 1995, Berkshire changed from a single County Council to six Unitary Councils and the Shire Hall was no longer required. The building was acquired by Digital Electronic Corporation (DEC), a computer company who moved from a smaller site at Basingstoke Road in Whitley Wood, and by 2000 the site had been acquired by Foster Wheeler, an oil and gas infrastructure supplies company, who moved there from its previous location on the former Vincent's garage site opposite the rail station in the town centre.

Shinfield Players Theatre

The Shinfield Players Theatre was started in 1956 and 17 years later opened a theatre at its present home off Whitley Wood Lane near the M4. In 2012 it was nominated for several awards by the National Operatic and Dramatic Association. The theatre building was previously the temporary NAAFI building in the RAF camp at Shinfield Park and was leased from the Meteorological Office after it had moved away. In 2014, the Players' committee was pursuing with the Met Office the possibility of an extended lease on the property and had a 10-year £1m plan which would be implemented, if that could be achieved, to provide a full redesign of the theatre and, if possible, a new purpose-built theatre building.

Chapter 8

Transport and Roads

Since early times, the Basingstoke Road (designated the A33 in the 20th century) was the main entry point from Southampton and Winchester in the south to Reading town, Oxford and further north. In the same way, the Shinfield Road (designated the A327) was the main route from Portsmouth, Aldershot and Farnborough. Until the early 20th century, the main transport was coach and horses or pony and trap. Then the advent of the motor vehicle (car, lorry and motor bus) meant that much more traffic was to be carried on these main roads and there was a growing need for improved roads both through Whitley and also around the south of Whitley as a bypass for Reading. Consequently, the late 20th century saw the construction of the M4 motorway and the A33 Relief Road.

Whitley Pump & Turnpike/Terminus

The Whitley Pump was erected at the top of Whitley Hill in the 19th century on the eastern corner of Whitley Street and Christchurch Road (then Whitley Crescent) to replace the King's Head Pond, both of which drew water from the surface gravel. The pond was so described because of its association with the public house, the King's Head, on the northern corner of what is now Milman Road. The pond made way for the construction of the Christchurch Gardens estate in the late 19th century. The pump was removed during the 1940s when a roundabout was installed in the middle of the junction as a terminus for the Reading Transport trolley buses – later extended into Whitley. A replica of the Pump was erected In 1999 on the roundabout as a reminder of the original watering place for the horses pulling heavy loads up the hill from the town or towards the town.

The following photograph, taken around 1910, shows the original Pump with Christ Church in the background. With seats around the nearby trees, it proved to be a pleasant place for men and women to meet or rest as well as for the horses to be watered. There were no traffic build-ups in those days though.

Reading Buses

When trams were in operation in the town, the route extended only as far as Whitley Street and not into Whitley itself. There was no public transport to and within Whitley, only that which passed through to locations beyond the boundary. However, once trolley buses and motor buses were introduced, the town routes were extended with three routes – trolley buses to the end of Northumberland Avenue with a terminus at the junction with Whitley Wood Road (Number 15), trolley buses to Whitley Wood with a terminus at the junction of the Engineers Arms roundabout (Number 16) and motor buses down Northumberland Avenue and up Cressingham Road to terminate at the junction with Staverton Road (Number 23). When they ceased to run in Reading in 1968, the trolley buses were replaced with motor buses. The Number 23 service no longer runs and the other two are called Numbers 5 and 6 respectively, comprising the 'Emerald' service.

While Number 5 still terminates at Whitley Wood Road, the Number 6 route has been extended to do a slight detour round the lower part of Whitley Wood to pass the Community Centre in Whitley Wood Lane. There is also a recent addition to the services in Whitley, the Number 9, which passes along Shinfield Road, through Cressingham Road and Buckland Road to Basingstoke Road and loops around Lower Whitley to go back up Northumberland Avenue then through Cressingham Road taking passengers past the Hospital to and from the town centre.

In the following photograph, taken around 1967, a trolley bus is manoeuvring around the roundabout in Northumberland Avenue before passing on towards St Agnes' Church which is to be seen in the distance. This was not a normal service bus as it is showing its destination as Manor House via Seven Sisters (in London)!

Separate bus services run along Shinfield Road and through the Whiteknights Park (University) to Earley. These were Numbers 20 and 21 but routes were recently adjusted and the services became Numbers 21 and 21a, the 'Claret' service.

Routes that have been added more recently are the 'Greenwave' services from the town to Kennet Island, Green Park, the Madejski stadium, Tesco Depot and the International Business Park and also to Mereoak beyond the Junction 11 of the M4.

M4 motorway

The M4 motorway from London to Bath was built during the late 1960s and early 1970s. It skirted the south of Reading with a major junction (Junction 11) constructed where it crossed the Basingstoke Road between Whitley Wood and Three Mile Cross. The Reading by-pass section of the motorway was completed and opened in December 1971. Access to Junction 11 was provided from the Shinfield Road via a new roundabout and an extension to Whitley Wood Lane.

A33 Relief Road

With an Inner Distribution Road encircling the centre of the town from 1989 and the M4 passing round the south of the town, the traffic along Basingstoke Road (A33) and the IDR quickly grew and an improved way of carrying that traffic was needed. The construction of the A33 Relief Road to provide that improvement was agreed and the new road linking Junction 11 of the M4 (Basingstoke Road) and the IDR was constructed by building a new road across the River Kennet/Foudry Brook flood plain and constructing new junctions on the IDR and into Berkeley Avenue.

The new road passed the Worton Grange brewery site, which had been built near the junction to relocate the Courage Ltd Berkshire Brewery and give easy access to the M4. The ends of Acre Road and Bennet Road and the end of the pre-existing Rose Kiln Lane were joined to it as the new road made its way through to the IDR. It routed to the west of Fobney Brook and on over the Kennet with a spur road to the west to join Berkeley Avenue and the A4. It was completed in 1999. The impact of this new road was to open the door for major new development of the surrounding Kennet Valley area. The International Business Park, Green Park, the Reading Gate Retail Park and the Madejski Stadium complex were quickly under way, with plans in hand for many more commercial developments and the Kennet Island housing estate. As part of the development of the A33 Relief Road, Imperial Way was cut through from Basingstoke Road at the Whitley Wood Lane/Holiday Inn roundabout.

Chapter 9

Education

The first school built in Whitley was the National School near the junction of Whitley Wood Lane and Basingstoke Road, opposite the Grenadier public house. It was erected originally for the Sunday education of the children of Whitley Wood and the surrounding farms under the jurisdiction of the recently-formed District of Christ Church. It was designed by Henry Woodyer, who was also the architect of Christ Church on Whitley Hill, and it was opened in 1860, having been funded approximately half-each by a Mr Grainger and the Rev. Fosbery of St Giles' Church. In 1897, the School Board was requested to look at additional provision in Lower Whitley but the extension of the voluntary school by its managers was deemed adequate to meet the growing need in that area. In the 1930s the school was closed, not long after the opening of the Ridgeway School at the other end of Whitley Wood on the Shinfield Rise estate.

This photograph, which was taken around 2013, shows the original 1860 school building which has been converted into cottages in recent years.

In 2003 a Whitley Excellence Cluster was formed as part of the Government Excellence in Cities initiative, combining Whitley schools 'to develop new ways of sharing activities and supporting pupils and their families'. It was awarded £1.5m over 3 years by the Education and Skills Department to raise education standards. This grouping proved to be successful and continued to function beyond the initial

period. The schools involved were Blagdon Nursery, Christ the King Primary, New Christchurch Primary, Geoffrey Field Primary schools, George Palmer Primary, Ridgeway Primary, Whitley Park Primary schools, Reading Girls' School and Thamesbridge College (later to be John Madejski Academy). This continued until

2011 through support from the Reading Borough Council and, when that ceased, the community formed an Aspire2 support group to continue the funding from then on.

Unfortunately, because of Ofsted's call for the return to special measures of the John Madejski Academy and the Reading Girls' School in 2016, a particular emphasis was put on the need for the Reading Borough Council to put more effort into improving performance of schools.

Hamlet of Whitley School

This is a curiosity which has not been resolved in recent times. There is a reference in Leslie Harman's book 'The History of Education in Reading' that says that this school was built. However, the only reference found in mid-19th century documents is one in the 1861 census which lists the School House for the Hamlet of Whitley School being in the area of what became the Christ Church Gardens estate around the corner of Southern Hill and Whitley Road. It could have been that one of the existing houses was designated for this purpose. Thereafter there is no reference to the school or the school house. Had it been planned as a school, with a school house allocated, at that time? Was the whole plan overtaken by events when it was agreed to build Christ Church in 1861/2 with the intention to build the Christ Church School shortly after? That has so far not been answered.

The image on the previous page is an architect's drawing of the planned school building as proposed in 1855 to Rev. Grainger, the Vicar of St Giles, before Christ Church itself was even considered. The original of this drawing is held by the Reading Central Library.

Blagdon Road Nursery School

This was opened in 1937 at the lower end of Blagdon Road, near Northumberland Avenue, in response to the increasing number of small children as Lower Whitley was expanding. It continues today as the Blagdon Nursery School and Children's Centre including Willows Day Nursery. In 2011 and 2014 it achieved an 'Outstanding' Ofsted rating.

The opening of the Nursery is shown in the following photograph. Making a speech is Nancy, Lady Astor, the first lady MP and resident of Cliveden House at Taplow. To her right is the Medical Officer of Health, Mr H J Milligan, and to her left is seated the Mayor, Mrs Alice Jenkins.

Abbey School - Junior School and Early Years Centre

The Abbey School opened a preparatory school for younger girls in 1905 at the Kendrick Road school buildings. In 1945 the school acquired Kensington House in Christchurch Road (a house originally designed by Alfred Waterhouse in around 1876) and this became the permanent home of the Junior School continuing to the present day.

Earlier, in 1923, the boarders had moved into the privately-owned Kensington House together with the Junior School and it was renamed Abbey House, though it was quickly restored to the building's former name. In 1926, the School obtained the use of 4 Christchurch Gardens for junior boarders and called it Burge House after the then Bishop of Oxford who had close links with the school. In 1928, these boarders along with the name of Burge House moved to the larger 12 Christchurch Gardens where it remained until 1933 when it was moved to 'Oakfield' at 48 Redlands Road until 1942. The school also owned houses in Christchurch Road, Erleigh Road and Maitland Road (off Tilehurst Road) for the use of boarders at various times prior to 1945 when it finally acquired Kensington House. At this time, boarding at the School ended and The Abbey School became a day-school only for girls. An extension was built on the west and south sides at Kensington House in the late 1990s.

In 2002, the Abbey School opened the former Christ Church Vicarage in Vicarage Road, another house originally designed by Waterhouse in around 1871, as an Early Years Centre for girls aged three-to-five years. The building is known as Knell House after Bishop of Reading Eric Knell and is shown in the 2016 photograph above.

During 2006, the Abbey School, having acquired and demolished the adjacent Two Ways Cottage property in Vicarage Road, added a new building, Somerleaze House, to its Junior School to house Years 5 and 6 together with a music department and an activity studio. 'Somerleaze' was the original name for Kensington House when it was first built.

In 2011, the School acquired No 12 Christchurch Gardens, formerly the Judge's lodgings and which had been used by the School previously between 1928 and 1933. This was re-developed as an extension to the Junior School and opened in October 2013 as The Abbey Gardens, for reception and Year 1 pupils.

George Palmer Schools / Cintra School

A pair of two-storey red brick buildings was erected off Basingstoke Road, adjacent to the grounds of Whitley Rise, during 1906 and 1907, giving a block of classrooms on each floor with halls and lobbies. In the autumn of 1907, George Palmer School was completed ready to take children from the Southampton Street School, formerly the British School. This was the first school built in Whitley after the old National School in Whitley Wood.

The Western Block, nearest to the Basingstoke Road entrance, housed the Infants' School (5-7 years) on the ground floor and the Girls' School (7-14 years) on the upper floor. The Eastern Block housed the Boys' School (7-14 years) on the ground floor and the Borough Pupil Teacher training centre (16-18 years) in preparation for teacher training college on the upper floor; upstairs was a Science room and below it an Arts Centre. In a separate building between the main blocks was a Domestic Science Centre and, beyond the Eastern Block, was a Manual Instruction Centre with workshops.

In 1912, the Pupil Teacher training centre was removed as arrangements for training had changed. A new Senior School was introduced in its place with classrooms, an arts centre, the 2 workshops and space for 300 pupils. Boys and girls from 13 years upwards were brought into the George Palmer Senior Preparatory Trade School from April that year. The boys were trained in brick building and other trades while the girls were trained in needlework, domestic science, etc.

During the Great War, Leonard Sutton allowed the George Palmer schools to use the playing fields in Cintra Park adjacent to Cintra Lodge.

1920 saw the change of name for the Senior School to the George Palmer Central School and Pupil Teacher training was reintroduced shortly afterwards (only to be removed again in 1925!).

Because of increasing demand with the growth of the Whitley estate, the George Palmer Senior Boys' Department was moved in 1930 from the Eastern Block to combine with the Senior Boys' Department at Katesgrove School. This then released space for the George Palmer Junior Mixed Department. The George Palmer Senior Girls' remained where they were in the Western Block and the Junior Mixed Department above the separate Infants Department in the Eastern Block. An ex-Army hut was erected next to the workshop centre to provide an arts centre to replace the original which had been taken over as a classroom and an extension was put up at the end of the Eastern Block with two classrooms one above the other for the Junior School. Then in 1934 the Central School took over the whole upper floor with the Juniors moving into the hut. The following year the Central School moved to a more academic approach with foreign language included for School Certificate requirement.

The following photograph shows the Eastern Block building in 2004 shortly before it was demolished.

The start of the Second World War resulted in more changes, firstly with evacuation plans arranged in August 1939 and then cancelled shortly afterwards. School meals were being provided in the British Restaurant in

Northumberland Avenue and were then, in 1943, brought into the school hall. The school playing field was used by Katesgrove boys to create a kitchen garden soon after the start of the war and then, in 1941, a piece of land at Whitley Rise was set aside for school gardening classes. Two air raid shelters were built. Once the war was over, a Junior School of Building was introduced in a new department for boys of 13 years and over. Instruction took place in Whitley Rise until huts were erected in place of the air raid shelters in 1948.

By 1950, there was much higher demand for secondary school places than before and the Senior School for Girls made use of the South Reading Community Centre (for the gymnasium and rooms) and the Whitley Rise house (for additional rooms) and its garden. Then, in 1952, some 300 boys from the George Palmer Central School moved to the newly-opened Ashmead School, further down in Northumberland Avenue. The George Palmer Central Girls' School combined with the Girls' Secondary Modern School to form the George Palmer Secondary Girls' School on a selective streamed basis, taking over the whole of the Western Block. That was the end of the Central School.

The 1950s saw the George Palmer Primary Schools obtain their own playing fields, adjacent to and sloping down from the school buildings, to replace the ones that had been used for many years in Cintra Park, though that was still used by the Seniors and later Cintra School. This happened just before the Home Farm estate was sold to the Council. The Selways, who owned the farm, gave the piece of land to the schools because of their close association with them.

It was all change again in 1960. The girls, mainly from the lower end of Whitley, who were attending George Palmer Secondary Girls' School in the Western Block, were moved down Northumberland Avenue and on the other side of the road to the new Southlands School when it opened in that autumn. The vacated school building was refurbished and the boys and girls of Katesgrove Secondary Modern School were moved that same year to form the new Cintra Secondary School on the George Palmer site in the Western Block. Thus children who had left George Palmer Junior and gone on to Katesgrove Secondary Modern had to move back to the George Palmer site as Cintra School pupils. This helped to share the load of the increasing numbers for secondary education in Whitley.

From the mid-1960s, the Junior School used the original Avenue School building in Northumberland Avenue as an Annexe and this continued until the late 1970s. The Cintra School finally closed in 1978 when its pupils were transferred to Long Lane Comprehensive School in Tilehurst. From then on, the School buildings were used for Infants and Juniors only, later being renamed the George Palmer Primary School.

In 2004, George Palmer Primary School's two old Edwardian buildings were demolished after a single, modern building had been built and opened on part of the same site to replace them. The photograph above shows the Eastern Block under demolition. The area left was redeveloped for housing (Scholar's Place), with work starting on this in 2006 and finished in 2008. In 2007, the George Palmer School celebrated its centenary. In 2010, the school was rated 'Satisfactory' by Ofsted. However, two years later, it was placed in special measures as standards had fallen to 'Inadequate' across the board and, consequently, it was proposed to re-open it as The Palmer Academy to give it a new start. This came to fruition in September 2013 and, at the same time, it joined the Reach2 Thames Valley Multi-Academy Trust.

This photograph shows the new George Palmer Primary School on the day of its official opening in 2004.

The Whitley Special School/Avenue School

Following the 1899 Act relating to 'Defective and Epileptic Children', 10 children were admitted to a Special Class 'for the training and education of Physically and Mentally Deficient Children' in Oxford Road School in September 1901 under Miss Sophy Allen. A Special Committee was established to oversee the school and that included Miss Edith Sutton (of the Sutton's Seeds family) and Mr Collier (of the Collier's Brick company) as well as a Visitor, Canon Ducat. Because of the growth in numbers in the next few years, the Special School was transferred to temporary location at Elm Park Wesleyan Hall in 1905. The following year some boys attended a centre at Battle School for instruction in woodwork, etc. But there was a clear need for a better site for the School, as stressed by the Inspectors in 1907, despite its good performance.

In 1909, the School at Elm Park was closed and a new School opened that September at a 2-acre site on Whitley Hill, the first building in the recently-created Northumberland Avenue. This 'School for Mentally and Physically Defective Children' was known as the Whitley Special School. The building had been designed by W R Howell in 1908. Dinners were provided for the children and, in 1910, there was capacity for a total of 100 children. It was decided that an open-air section, a 'Phthisical School' was required for use by those suffering from pulmonary tuberculosis and other breathing-related problems. An annexe was built and opened on the west side in mid-1911. This section became known as the Open Air School because it could be opened up to teach the children on the verandah outside – at all times of the year – to take advantage of the (then) fresh open air on the top of the hill.

Not long after the Open Air School was opened, the photograph on the following page was taken. It shows the building with all the doors open to give the maximum airing, several teachers and a group of children in their school uniforms, some sitting on chairs, some on the ground and one of them on a bed.

With the start of the War in 1939, the school was closed at the end of August to prepare for the arrival of evacuee children from London. This period of the Second War is described in the following:

On August 28, 1939, the school reopened after the summer break as normal but three days later the school closed after the afternoon session to prepare for the arrival of evacuee children from London. On September 2 1939, the school opened as an emergency billet and at 930pm 60 women and babies arrived. On

the next day, the PD department was opened as a treatment and observation centre. On December 25 that year, there were 26 evacuated children in residence for Christmas and various festivities were arranged for them. Many children and mothers with babies passed through over the following months until closure of the emergency billet was made on March 9 1940. In that time, 396 evacuees passed through the school comprising 56 women, 113 accompanied children and 227 unaccompanied children. The school was closed from March 9 until April 1 1940 for cleaning and decorating, during which period the school children were transferred to 44 Christchurch Road. When it reopened on April 1, there were 104 children present.

During the remainder of the war, the school experienced a few air raid warnings. On 5 and 6 September 1940, the sirens sounded in the morning and the school children proceeded to the shelters in an orderly manner with all-clear sounded around half-an-hour later. On January 28 1941, the siren sounded just as school was closing at 330pm; A busload of children were despatched on their way and the remainder were taken to the school air raid shelter.

[Summarised from entries in the log books of 'The Avenue School', by kind permission of Dame Sue Bourne, Head Teacher.]

The 1944 Education Act extended the scope of Special Schools and allowed Special Educational Treatment to be provided other than at schools – hospitals, etc. - for those with severe problems.

In 1951, the School formally changed its name to The Avenue School, with three Departments – Educationally Sub-Normal, Physically Handicapped and Open Air. In the 1950s the school site was extended to the west to provide a playing field. Then the Council agreed for the site of the old 'Whitley Rise' house and its grounds to be cleared to allow a new extension to the school to be built. Although a cottage and some garages were retained on the site, the new building was completed in 1957 and opened in January 1958 with a pathway around the playing fields linking the western and eastern parts of the School.

The photograph below is of the Open Air School at a much later date than the previous one, probably in the 1950s. There are many more children, the ones closest are on metal-framed beds with canvas to lay on, girls in one row and boys in another, and all facing the same way to benefit from the open air in the sunshine. There is a nurse in view who is in charge of the children.

In 1965 the foundation stone for another new building was laid by 'Mr Pastry' (children's favourite Richard Hearne), and he returned to open the completed new swimming pool facility in 1967.

By 1967 the Open Air School extension was demolished as the incidence of tuberculosis had reduced greatly. The original building facing Northumberland Avenue was used, from the mid-1960s, as an Annexe by George Palmer Junior School. By the late 1970s the Avenue School needed the space back at the Northumberland Avenue building for its own use to cater for the growth in numbers.

The following photograph, taken in 2007, shows the Northumberland Avenue building from the inner playground. The paint on the left hand wall is a remnant from where the Open Air School building had previously stood. The hexagonal roof on the small extension in the middle with the tall chimney by it is interesting. Note also the bell housing on the main roof which is very similar to that on the George Palmer Eastern Block roof.

At its peak there were some 275 children at the School. The vast majority of children came from Reading but a significant number came from other parts of Berkshire and beyond, even though there were two other special needs schools in the area (Woodley and Tilehurst). Many children were brought to the School and taken home on coaches. An additional sign of change at the School had been that the number of spina bifida children had decreased while the number of autistic children had grown which required different kinds of facilities and teaching practices.

Relocation of the Avenue Special School to a new site elsewhere in the town was considered by the Council for several years. It was decided and confirmed in

2006 that this move would be to the former Meadway School site in Tilehurst, which was to be redeveloped as part of a £13m scheme, and the move took place in September 2008.

The original Avenue School building just survived to reach its 100th birthday in 2009 when the whole of the school's site was under redevelopment and the old building was demolished that year. In 2010, work started on redevelopment of the whole site for housing and a care home, which was completed in 2013.

In 2013, Sue Bourne, the Head Teacher, was made a Dame in the Queen's Birthday Honours after ten very successful years in the post.

Wakefield Lodge/Reading Alternative School/Phoenix College

As part of the development of 'special school' provision in the town in the early 1900s, Reading provided an Occupation Centre for young people who needed extra tuition to assist them in obtaining and keeping jobs in the community. The first location of this centre was at St Laurence's Church in 1929, moving to Watlington House two years later. By 1947, it had outgrown the facilities there and was moved to 'The Beeches' at 109 London Road. This building had previously been used as St Andrew's Hostel for University College students and then as a Council-run Children's Care Home. Finally, in 1957, the Centre moved to Ashton Lodge, a house in Christchurch Road, which had been renamed Wakefield Lodge. This facility was called the Reading Borough Training Centre and was set up to help mentally handicapped youngsters. It opened with 18 young people moving from The Beeches in London Road, quickly increasing to 32. The Beeches has since been demolished and replaced with a block of flats.

The name of the Reading Borough Training Centre at Wakefield Lodge in Christchurch Road was changed to the Wakefield Lodge Special School and it continued in that form for more than twenty years until 1981 when it was closed. It then re-opened as the Reading Alternative School in 1983 for children with behavioural, social and emotional problems, who could not cope with normal secondary education. A warden was to be on site and there were ten beds for overnight stay and a total of 40 places for these youngsters in the 14 to 16 age range.

The Reading Alternative School was given a makeover following poor reports from Ofsted in 2000 and 2004. In December 2005, it was re-branded as the Phoenix College with a new approach to the specialist training of these young people with complex educational needs. It received a good report in 2006 thus appearing to have made a start in 'rising from the ashes'.

The photograph below shows the Phoenix College as it was in 2016.

Because of the increasing number of students at this college, it was agreed with the Council in 2014 that the Cintra Park Pavilion could be used to give extra space – the pavilion would still be open to the public outside school hours. In 2011 and 2014, it continued to achieve 'Good' ratings from Ofsted.

Ridgeway Primary School

In 1925, a build-up started of children attending the Redlands Schools from the new Council estate at Shinfield Rise in Whitley. The increasing number at Redlands, as well as the fact that it was a fairly long walk to get to Redlands School for children from the new estate, caused some concerns. Initially it was suggested that St. Barnabas Church Hall be used but the Board of Education decided on a site in Willow Gardens. The land was donated by Mr. Kingham on condition that no building took place behind Hazel Crescent for 25 years. To achieve this condition, access by vehicles was only permitted via Willow Gardens, with a footway through from Whitley Wood Road.

The new Primary School was erected in the Shinfield Rise estate in 1929 and was called the Shinfield Road Council School with around 350 children, divided into Infants, Junior Boys and Junior Girls. The design was by Charles Smith and Son, the local architects. The school was further extended in 1931 to increase the capacity. When Geoffrey Field School opened in 1949 (Infants) and 1951 (Juniors), this relieved the increasing growth at the Shinfield Road School. Separate school dining facilities were built in 1949. Previously, school dinners had been provided in the school hall. Most children went on to the George Palmer Central School, very few being selected for the grammar schools. The name of the school was changed in 1951 to Ridgeway School in order to offset confusion with the Shinfield Village School. A larger playing field was acquired by purchasing the adjacent 4 acre field in 1957.

Ridgeway Primary School was rated 'Good' in February 2013, an improvement on its 'Satisfactory' rating in 2011.

In 2014, plans were being considered for a revamping of the school with upgrades to existing buildings and addition of a new two-storey block for extra classrooms and other facilities. This also proposed that the main entrance to the school would be via Hillbrow, off Whitley Wood Road, instead of Willow Gardens. The work was completed in late 2016 allowing an increase in capacity to 630 pupils and the new buildings opened in November that year.

Whitley Park Primary and Nursery School

The Whitley Park schools (Junior and Infant/Nursery) were built in 1934. They provided for the growing number of children in the middle part of Whitley.

Whitley Park Infant and Nursery School was rated 'Outstanding' in all respects in 2009, its 75th anniversary year but within a few years was rated 'Inadequate'.

The Infant and Nursery School and the Junior School agreed to merge into a single school in 2010 with massive support from parents and teachers alike. It was renamed Whitley Park Primary and Nursery School. New facilities were also opened in 2011 for an Early Years Centre.

Ian Waite, the dancer, of TV programme 'Strictly Come Dancing' fame and Ricky Gervais, the comedian, of TV programmes 'The Office' and 'Extras' fame both attended this school.

Geoffrey Field Primary School

Geoffrey Field Primary School opened in 1949 with an Infant Department for 240 pupils and the Junior Department followed in 1951 as part of the

Education Committee's post-war plan to address the rapid growth in intake since the Second World War. It completed the provision of primary education in Whitley.

In 1981 a playgroup was opened and followed with a nursery unit in 1983. This gave an improved pre-school education in Lower Whitley.

Geoffrey Field Infants School in Exbourne Road was deemed 'Outstanding' in July 2008 followed by the Junior School, which was rated 'Good' overall and 'Outstanding' in many parts, later that year. The Infants School repeated its success in July 2013.

Christ the King Catholic Primary School

Christ the King Primary School was opened on 3rd July 1968 in Lulworth Road, Whitley, to serve the Catholic families of Whitley. It was built using donations and funds raised by the Church. When St James' School in the town closed down at about the same time, its children also joined Christ the King School.

A well–known footballer who attended the school in the 1960s is Lawrie Sanchez, who played for Reading FC before moving on to Wimbledon FC and later went on to be the successful manager of the Northern Ireland national team.

In March 2010, the Christ the King Voluntary-Aided Catholic Primary announced that it planned to open a specialist autism unit supporting up to 10 children with Autism Spectrum Disorders at a cost of some £750,000. It was to be aimed at children from across the Borough in particular. The proposal was approved in January 2011 and the specialist unit was opened in November 2011. Specialist secondary provision was at Blessed Hugh Faringdon School in Southcote. In 2014, a £10,000 special sensory room was opened for the use of the autistic children.

Southlands School/Reading Girls School

In 1960, Southlands School opened in Northumberland Avenue as a girls' secondary modern school to replace George Palmer Secondary Girls' Department, serving the major part of the Whitley area. It was built to provide accommodation for 600 to 700 girls in a four-form entry providing at least two alternative courses.

It was proposed that it change to co-educational secondary with Ashmead in 1989, following the merger of their sixth forms in 1984, but there was great objection to going down that path and eventually, in 1992, Ashmead changed to co-education on its own. Meanwhile Southlands opted out of local authority control and changed to a grant-maintained girls' comprehensive school in 1990. In 1993 the name of the school was changed to Reading Girls' School and remained the only all-girls comprehensive in Reading, with an intake coming from the whole of the Reading area. Selective streaming was introduced in the same year within the comprehensive system.

Reading Girls' School was put on special measures in 2005 after being declared a failing school and then taken off in June 2006, though its sixth form provision was considered inadequate. In 2007, Mrs Marsha Elms of Kendrick School was brought in as executive head for the school, as part of a Kendrick Federation, and plans were prepared for a new £3m sixth-form centre. This new centre was

completed and opened in September 2009. The centre was initially managed by the Thames Valley University as part of a plan to improve standards at the school, though this was taken over by the Reading College in 2010. Up to 176 students could take A-levels, GCSE re-sits, NVQ courses, etc. and the two-storey building included a nursery for parents to leave children while they study. In 2010, the school, shown in the photograph above, which was taken in 2017, also celebrated its 50th year.

The Girls' School itself later became a Foundation School, specialising in Business and Enterprise, and changed to be partially selective providing both academic and vocational educational options. Mrs Elms retired in March 2012 having achieved a 'good' Ofsted rating for Reading Girls' School.

In 2013, it was announced that the School (excluding the Sixth Form Centre, since named the Northumberland Training Academy) would be renovated by completely replacing the school buildings on the site. This would allow an increase in the capacity from 700 to 1050 students from September 2016, the £26m reconstruction starting in late 2014 once the plans had gained approval by the Borough Council. The new school was also expected to provide 18 work placements and 40 apprenticeships for local residents.

The following photograph shows the Training Academy frontage, taken in 2017.

Unfortunately the School's Ofsted rating slipped to 'Inadequate' in early 2016 and that was going to need some quick work to remedy the failing aspects of its performance. It was earmarked for conversion to Academy status.

Ashmead Secondary School/Thamesbridge College/John Madejski Academy

Ashmead School was opened in 1951/52 to serve the Whitley area as a Technical School, one of the three categories of secondary school that had been introduced under the 1944 Education Act. It took over from George Palmer Central School in providing a building school covering plumbing, bricklaying, carpentry and science. The school was built in Northumberland Avenue, on the corner of Hartland Road, and was proud of its record of excellence for many years. Its role as a technical school, in spite of its success, was changed to that of a standard secondary modern school by the end of the 1950s. It became Ashmead Comprehensive School in the 70s and, sadly, the performance and consequently the school's reputation deteriorated in the 80s and it became a real struggle to improve performance over some 20 years.

By 1989, there was a move to convert Ashmead and its associate girls' school in Whitley, Southlands, into a single co-educational comprehensive secondary after a merger of their sixth forms in 1984. However, this was not approved and, instead, Ashmead went on to become co-educational on its own from September 1992 as Ashmead Community School. The poor performance continued however and, in 1998, Ofsted gave the school a 'failing' assessment. This prolonged period of being seen as the school at the bottom of those in Berkshire was demoralising for teachers and pupils alike. Then Marsha Elms, the Head of Kendrick School, was brought in for a short period to try and turn performance around in the spring of 1998. A new Head was appointed in September 1998 (Caroline James) and by July 2000 the school was taken off special measures. At the start of the September 2000 school year, it re-opened as Thamesbridge College. Plans had been approved for improvements and some of the old original buildings were demolished to make way for a new science block and a sixth form centre. Expectations were raised that the school was on the way up.

The former Ashmead School has lived through several transformations in its 50 and more years. Its existence as Thamesbridge College came to an end after Ofsted reported serious weaknesses in 2003. The College ceased to exist in 2006 after its re-opening that September as Reading's first City Academy, the John Madejski Academy, which had a sports specialism and much improved facilities. The aim was to provide a good local comprehensive school with emphasis on sport and at full capacity would take 1100 students. The new buildings were finished at the end of that year with the move into them taking place in readiness for January 2007. The official opening of the £27m development took place in February 2007. Interest in this alternatively-focussed curriculum encouraged more pupils to apply for places and many people were watching closely to see if the school's poor performance in its recent past was turned round permanently in its new guise.

The results in 2008 were encouraging and much improved (25% getting five or more A*-C GCSE results including English and Maths). The first full Ofsted report gave a 'Good' assessment overall. However, in 2012, the school was put on 'Special Measures' but improved to gain a 'Good' rating in 2013 with the new Head Teacher aiming for an 'Outstanding' rating by 2016. In 2014, work started on a £1m improvement of its sixth-form centre, providing better facilities including an 80-seater drama studio, opening in early 2015. However, in 2016, it was announced by Ofsted that the school was dropped to 'special measures' status again.

The following photograph shows the Hartland Road entrance to the modern buildings of the Academy .

Shortly after its opening, the Academy also took over the former South Reading Leisure Centre in Rabson's Recreation Ground. This leisure centre had been provided on the playing fields left by John Rabson for public use. The JMA Trust proposal to the Council that the Academy should run the leisure centre raised concerns that it was going to affect users of the gym and swimming pool, which were used by children's groups and the Over 50s Club. To address concerns, the South Reading Leisure Centre was then re-opened for shared public and school use and renamed the Academy Sport Leisure Centre.

Leighton Park School

Early in the 19th century the Society of Friends took the decision to build its own schools to overcome the difficulties encountered by having to send their children to either church schools or public schools. The first to be founded by the Quakers was the Grove House School in Tottenham, London, which was erected in 1828. However, after some fifty years, the school was closed and sold off to the last headmaster. The funds obtained from the sale were then used to restart at a new location. This was chosen to be Leighton Park in 1889, the site being a 40 acre park with a 19th century house that was known locally as Pepper Manor, from which the name of the adjacent Pepper Lane was taken. In 1890, the school re-opened here with a new headmaster and four boys. The house was named Grove House after its Tottenham predecessor and was extended to cater for further Quaker boys.

By 1894 a second boarding house was opened (designed by Alfred Waterhouse, a Quaker and relative of a Governor). This brought the total capacity of the boarding school up to 46 boys and, with a swimming bath added, that completed the building work until the next century. Further buildings were then added in 1915 and 1920 bringing the capacity up to 103 boys.

1924 saw the School purchase Cressingham Park, an adjacent property in Shinfield Road which had previously been owned by the Lonergan family since the late 19th century. Another school boarding house was created in this newly acquired land, by converting Cressingham House.

A change of headmaster and introduction of day-boarders increased the number of boys attending the school to more than 200 by the end of the Second World War. The school was now well recognised for its approach and achievements.

In 1972, a new £150,000 hall and music school was opened. Then, in 1975 girls were included in the sixth form as day-boarders. It was planned to move to co-education at a later date. The starting age had been 13 years but in 1985 this was reduced to 11 years to align with general secondary school practice. The following year a new phase of development was commenced because of the deterioration of the School House and to provide a new swimming pool. To fund this, some 10 acres of the old Cressingham Park land was sold off for £7.5m in 1988, including the old house, and was developed into what became Devonshire Park estate. To compensate for the loss of the building, a new house was erected in the remaining parkland of the school. In September 1993, the school changed to full co-education.

Famous old boys of the school are Michael Foot, the former Labour party leader, and film directors Sir David Lean and Karl Reisz.

In 1940, Leighton Park established a Junior School by taking over the Marlborough House Preparatory School.

Crosfields School

Originally the Marlborough House Preparatory School for Boys in Castle Street, Reading, dating back to the early 19th century, and following moves to Bath Road and Parkside Road, the school was taken under the wing of the Leighton Park School in 1940 as Leighton Park Junior School. The 'Goodrest' Estate, a 66-acre property on the hill by Shinfield Road and overlooking the Whitley lower level, was bought as a suitable location for the school in 1946. It had been used as a RAF Officers' Convalescent Home during the war. In 1957, the school was opened on a non-profit Trust basis independent of Leighton Park School though still retaining links between the two schools. The name was changed to Crosfields in memory of Hugh Crosfield, a former Governor, who had been killed in 1944.

In the 1950s the numbers of pupils, day and boarder, grew to around 100 boys and this increased to 180 boys by the 1960s. A Headmaster's house was built in the 1960s and was named 'Goodrest'. During the 1970s, a new kitchen was built and part of the estate (the lake and cedar trees) was sold enabling a new Junior School and other facilities to be built. The original buildings (the White Building and its Stable Block) continued as the main school buildings, though a number of new buildings were added during the following years, including the Music Block, the Gymnasium, The Chestnuts reception block and The Acorns for years 1-4. 2007 saw the school celebrate its 50th year with a new building, The Oaks, completed (after demolition of the old Stable Block) and opened by the Bishop of Reading, Stephen Cottrell. The Oaks opened with many new facilities including extra classrooms, art studio, library, design workshop and ICT facilities. Girls were admitted into the Years One and Two (Pre-preparatory) from September 2007 and in full from 3 to 13 from September 2008; ballet and dance were included in the curriculum.

The photograph above shows the White Building, the 19th century version of 'Goodrest', as it was in 2014.

Pinecroft and White Barn Care Homes

The Cressingham Children's Home at Pinecroft in Monksbarn, off Cressingham Road, provides continuing care for children up to 18 years with physical and learning problems and needing round the clock support. In recent years, this has been considered for an extension to its role to include working with the Avenue School in providing respite care for Autistic children. The home run by Reading Council was judged to be 'Outstanding' by Ofsted in 2016 for a second successive year.

The White Barn at 45a Cressingham Road is run by the Kingwood Trust. It provides residential care for four people of 18+ years of age and also day care. It caters for adults with autism and autistic spectrum disorders.

Elm House Remand Home

At the corner of Whitley Wood Road and Basingstoke Road there used to stand a house called Elm House, formerly known as The Elms. After the Second War, this house was used by the Reading Borough as a Remand Home under the Children's Department.

Chapter 10

Places of Worship

Prior to the building of the Whitley Wood School Church and Christ Church on Whitley Hill, there were two churches available to residents of Whitley – St Giles' in Southampton Street and St John's in Watlington Street.

Christ Church

Around the end of the 18th century, the inhabitants of the hamlet and Manor of Whitley had tried to get a separate parish established for their locality thus reversing the status that had existed from the Middle Ages whereby Whitley was made part of the parish of St Giles' Church. This bid for separation was unsuccessful though some concessions were made allowing certain rights. Consequently, 'preaching stations' were established. The tenure of Rev. Fosbery at St Giles' Church led to a revisit to this claim and a desire by the hamlet and other local residents for a new church to be built.

Further concessions were made and Sir William Milman donated suitable land that was opposite the top of the Kendrick Road and alongside Southern Hill. Gifts were made by an unnamed priest of £4000 and by the Church Commissioners of £3000 to cover the costs. Bishop Wilberforce laid a foundation stone for the daughter church, to be called Christ Church, on July 7th 1861. The new church building, which was consecrated on August 7th 1862, was designed by Henry Woodyer (also architect of St Paul's Wokingham) and it consisted of a nave, chancel, north aisle, side chapel (the 'Lady Chapel') and a vestry. The building was of brick faced with flint and stone and dressed with Bath stone, described as being Decorated Gothic.

Christ Church had been intended as a Chapel of Ease to St Giles' Church *but the munificence of a clergyman afforded an opportunity of procuring its independent endowment as a separate District Church.* (From "Parish of St Giles-in-Reading" by Leslie Harman). Thus the people of Whitley hamlet achieved their aim of a separation from St Giles'. The first vicar of the parish was Rev. W. Addison whose endowment came from Rev. D. Beaufort and the Church Commissioners. A Church vicarage was built in around 1871 to a design by Alfred Waterhouse and this continued to serve the parish until around 1977 when a new modern vicarage was built in the grounds of the old house. The old vicarage was later acquired by The Abbey School for its Early Years Centre and opened in 2002.

The photograph below shows the original church building in the 1860s without the spire and with only the start of a tower. The street wall along the frontage is just the same today.

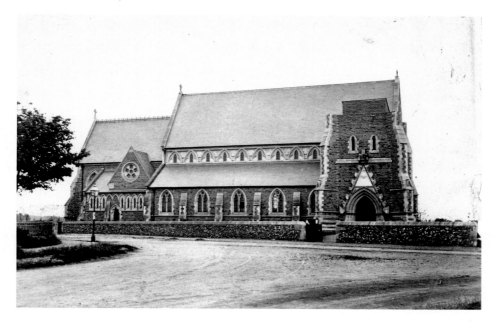

By 1874, there was a need to enlarge the Church and Henry Woodyer took on the task of designing a substantial extension to allow a south aisle, a tower, spire and choir vestry to be added at a cost of £4000. The church was designed to hold 700 people and the added tower was topped with a stone spire of some 150 feet in height, which is clearly visible for some distance across the river valleys and to the motorway and beyond, the most prominent spire of the town of Reading. It contains an almost complete set of original Victorian stained glass windows (one or two have been damaged and replaced in recent times).

A church school was opened in 1868 as Christ Church School in what was to become Milman Road, named after Sir William Milman. This school was enlarged in 1883. It catered for boys, girls and infants.

There are two bells at Christ Church, the smaller chiming bell was cast in 1862 for the original church and the larger clock bell was cast in 1891, both by J Warner & Son of London. The war memorial in the front lawn was designed by W.R. Howell and erected in 1920 to commemorate the fallen of the parish from the Great War.

In 1945, Rev. Eric Knell was appointed as Vicar. From 1955, he was also Bishop of Reading and Archdeacon of Berkshire. He continued until he retired in 1962.

For many years, in the second half of the 20th century, the male choir at Christ Church was renowned for its performance of a wide range of choral music. It was invited to sing at other churches and at cathedrals under Leslie Davis, who was the organist and choirmaster from 1952 to 1995, a total of 43 years until he retired. More recently, invitations have continued with the Church's mixed choir.

The following photograph shows the Christ Church choir with the vicar, Rev John Deuchar. This was taken at Guildford Cathedral in 1980 before the choir sang a special evensong service.

Another role of Christ Church during the mid-20th century was that of University church with the Anglican chaplain under its wing. This meant that there were strong links between the University and Christ Church.

Around 1980, a major extension was undertaken by public subscription to allow a meeting room with a gallery above it, a kitchen and toilets to be added at the rear of the church; this required major surgery to the west end of the nave to open up the space for the additional facilities and provide access. Rev. Eric Essery became Vicar in 1984 and was appointed a Canon and then Rural Dean of Reading before he retired in 1999.

In 2001 an appeal was launched to obtain the funds needed to restore the church fabric as the roof and some of the pinnacles and gargoyles were in need of repair or replacement in order to prevent serious damage or injury arising. The work was completed after a few years with the help of grants and public subscriptions.

From its creation, Christ Church parish covered the whole of Whitley, including initially the Lower Whitley mission church, also designed by Henry Woodyer, and later the districts of St Agnes' Church and St Paul's Church (the latter had replaced the Lower Whitley Church). The parish was divided in the 1980s to separate Christ Church from the other two, which became the Lower Whitley parish and later included St Barnabas' Church in Elm Road.

St Agnes' Church

Money was collected for a church in Silver Street at the beginning of the 20th century. Dedicated to St Agnes in April 1904, it replaced an iron mission room. When the Silver St neighbourhood was partially cleared, the vicar of St Giles' Church closed the church of St Agnes and gave the furniture to a new church building on Lower Whitley estate, also to be called St Agnes. The use of the former building in Silver St changed to occasional social and educational work. St Agnes' Church in Northumberland Avenue was completed and dedicated on June 24th 1939, celebrating its 75th year in 2014. It has one bell which was originally hung in the Silver Street church and later moved. Since the 1980s it has been the lead church in the parish covering the Whitley Group of Churches, its Vicar currently being Rev. Vernon Orr. The church as it is today is shown in the following photograph, taken in 2017.

Lower Whitley Church/St Paul's Church

To meet the needs of the rural section of the St Giles' parish, a new School House was erected in Lower Whitley for Divine Service on Sundays. The decision for this took place in the mid-19th century. It was opened in 1860 by Archdeacon Randall. The School House was built of flint, dressed with Bath stone in Gothic style, and was partly provided by Mr Grainger (about half) and the rest came from Rev. Fosbery of St Giles' (£1028). The design was by Henry Woodyer who also designed Christ Church. The school was then used as a parish church for Lower Whitley from a little time afterwards, with regular Sunday services. In 1862, it became part of the new parish of Christ Church, which had then been separated from St Giles' parish.

St Paul's Mission Church was designed by W. R. Howell in 1911 and it opened in 1913 to replace the original School House. It has continued to serve the Whitley Wood community to the present day though there have been discussions about replacing it with a 'permanent' building that can also be used as a community centre. There are clearly difficulties with keeping church buildings independent and that has been evident at St Paul's Church in Lower Whitley. In late 2007, plans were unveiled for demolition of the church and its church hall (which is at present in a separate brick-built building) and replace them with a state-of-the-art medical and community centre together with a café, church and counselling centre. The whole proposal, which was put forward jointly by St Paul's Church, South Reading Surgery and the New Hope charity, was subject to consultation. There was no work undertaken following the publicity of the plans in 2007 because of lack of funding but, in 2013, it was announced that the development was being resurrected.

This photograph shows the church building in around 2010.

After the erection of the iron mission church of St Paul in 1913, the old School House building was used as the Church Hall for various local activities, home in the 1960s of a Youth Club and a scout group and various other community groups. More recently the building was converted into cottages.

St Barnabas' Church was erected in 1925 with 250 seats and is located near the corner of Elm Road with Shinfield Road. It became a District Church in 1938. Today it is part of the Whitley Group of Churches along with St Agnes' and St Paul's. It has one bell, cast in 1935 by Gillett & Johnson of Croydon.

The Bourne Memorial Methodist Church was opened in 1948 to meet the anticipated needs of the Whitley estate as it was being developed. This church was located in Exbourne Road and was a bright and airy centre at which the local Sunday School and Boys' Brigade flourished. Its Sunday services were initially well attended but this fell away over the 1960s and 70s until, in 1980, the church was closed as vandalism and disuse took its toll.

Christ the King Catholic Church
This was originally established as a daughter church of St James' in Forbury Road in the town centre to serve the Whitley Catholics. It used a wartime hut in Shinfield Road and a Scout hut in Callington Road for services and Sunday School. In 1946 St James' parish was divided and Christ the King became a separate parish with its own parish priest, Father Collins. Sisters from the St Joseph's Convent School were active in the parish, running Sunday School and preparing children for the sacraments. Having outgrown the huts, the church temporarily used the South Reading Community Centre until a new brick building in Cressingham Road had been erected in 1950 on land which was owned by the Church. This was an enormous task undertaken by a wide range of local people on a voluntary basis in their spare time and in the evenings after a day's work.

Every Spring, the annual May procession could be seen coming down Cressingham Road with the statue of the Virgin Mary being carried at the front and young girls dressed all in white, some with veils, following behind. At the bottom of Cressingham Road, the procession would walk along Northumberland Avenue before finally returning to the church, while local people would watch as they passed by.

A new church was built several years later on the corner of Brayford Road and Northumberland Avenue. It was consecrated in 1959, the foundation stone having been laid on October 25th, 1958. It became the centre of a flourishing parish, with its own school (now Christ the King Catholic Primary School) that was established in 1968. The old church building in Cressingham Road was used for many years as a church hall and later demolished. Father Collins was the parish priest for Christ the King Church for nearly 25 years (1946-1970) and was greatly appreciated for leading the parish through all its changes. The 50th anniversary of the Northumberland Avenue church was celebrated in 2008. This parish has been linked with St John Bosco Church parish in Woodley.

The following photograph of the church was taken in 2016.

Whitley Methodists moved to the Avenue School building in Northumberland Avenue after Whitley Hall in Whitley Street had closed in 1997 and moved on again to the Northcourt Avenue Scout and Guide building in 2008 after The Avenue School closed that year.

The well (formerly the Whitley Community Church) is situated at the rear of 29 Dawlish Road, backing on to the South Reading Community Centre. A church was first started here in a wooden hut as the Underwood Gospel Hall around the start of the Second World War. It continued with that name until the late 1970s when it became the Underwood Mission Hall with a new brick-built church building.

The Whitley Community Church started meeting at the South Reading Community Centre in the 1990s and later moved into the Underwood Mission Hall, taking its name with it to serve all the people of the local community. The church changed its name to 'the well' in 2010.

Reading Family Church meets on a Sunday at Reading Girls' School in the morning and at South Street Arts Centre in the evening. It was founded by a group of people from Bracknell in 2001. It has its administrative offices in London Street opposite Church Street.

Tyndale Baptist Church is situated in Cressingham Road near the junction with Shinfield Road. It is a multi-cultural family church and the building was erected in 1925.

Whitley Wood Reformed Baptist Church, formally established in 1994, meets at the Whitley Wood Community Centre in Copenhagen Close and holds Sunday School for children and also Adult meetings, both on a Sunday.

Reading Buddhist Priory is situated at 176 Cressingham Road, near the Whitley Library, and opened in 1990 as a local centre for the Order of Buddhist Contemplatives.

Chapter 11

Recreation and Entertainment

Finding ways of occupying spare time or places to enjoy watching or participating in sport or other means of entertainment have been a need of the Whitley community, as with any community, as it has expanded from its small beginnings in the 19th century through to today's large population in the 21st century. In the early years, with the peripheral residences located around the farmland, these were provided by the few cafes, beer houses and public houses in the area and also by Reading's own entertainment houses - the theatres and institutions, such as those in London Street and the town centre. There was, of course, ready access to the various open spaces along the rivers and other facilities such as sporting at Palmer Park and the Reading Football Club at Elm Park in West Reading. Transport was by horse and cart to start with and then by tram and later by 'bus or car to access the town. Today, public transport by 'bus is readily available from all parts of Whitley residential areas (Shinfield Road, Northumberland Avenue and Whitley Wood) and also the commercial areas to the west (Green Park and the Madejski Stadium Park and Ride).

Later, as the development of Whitley expanded rapidly in the 20th century, community centres were established. The South Reading Community Centre was opened in Northumberland Avenue around the time of the Second World War. This was more recently known as the South Reading Youth and Community Centre and it provides a Youth Club, a home for the Reading Karate Club and other facilities for all ages. Later in the 20th century, another community centre was established in the Swallowfield Drive estate in Whitley Wood, offering a range of activities including the hosting of a Youth Club and the Whitley Wood Baptist Church.

There is a Scout and Guide Hut in Northcourt Avenue, home of the 52nd Reading Scout Group which was registered in 1925. The 47th Reading (St Paul's) Scout Group, based at its own Scout Hut at the Whitley Wood Recreation Ground, celebrated its centenary in 2012.

Recreation Grounds in Whitley

With the size of the Whitley area, it was necessary to provide an increasing number of recreation areas to meet the needs of the population as it grew. Several were created when former farm land was left for this purpose as development of the Whitley Estate continued.

Cintra Park Recreation Ground, the land surrounding the former Cintra Lodge, was bequeathed to the town by Leonard Goodhart Sutton after his death in 1932 and ownership passed to the Council 25 years later. It was developed with football pitches, athletics track, cricket pitch, children's playground, tennis courts, a pavilion and a bowling green. Late in the 20th century the bowling green was closed; however, there were good alternative facilities available at Reading Bowling Club in Kendrick Road, the University of Reading Bowling Club and Whiteknights Indoor Bowling Club. Over many years, the Park has been used for local football matches.

The photograph is understood to show ladies taking tea after playing tennis in Cintra Park in around 1912 with men playing on the court in the background. The park was still privately owned at that time.

Long Barn Lane Recreation Ground was already used as a Children's Playground well before Home Farm was sold and the land was developed as a housing estate. It now contains a BMX track as well as the children's playground.

Rabson's Park Recreation Ground was a large piece of land left when the housing estates were developed along Northumberland Avenue and it sits between Blagdon Road and Hartland Road on the lower slope of the hill. It was named after Alderman John Rabson. This park includes the former South Reading Leisure Centre, now the Academy Sports Centre, and has also been used for local football matches for a long time.

Whitley Wood Recreation Ground was similarly left from former farm land as commercial development of the Whitley Wood end of Basingstoke Road took place near the Grenadier public house (now a Holiday Inn).

Reading Football Club and the Madejski Stadium

Reading Football Club, which was founded in 1871, started life using various local grounds for its home matches until it acquired its permanent home at Elm Park in Tilehurst in 1896. There it stayed for more than a hundred years. However, once John Madejski had bought the Club in 1990, he started work on finding a suitable new location for the football ground because Elm Park, with its capacity of 14,000 standing, was becoming more and more unsuitable as a location for a football stadium, particularly since the traffic congestion, difficulty of access and lack of parking restricted the ability to create an environment for a modern football club with aspirations to reach the Premier League.

In 1998, he opened a smart new 24,000 all-seat stadium having acquired the site of the former Smallmead civic amenity and it was named the Madejski Stadium. It was accompanied by an adjoining hotel, the Millennium Madejski Hotel, and a Conference Centre. It was agreed that the Reading Football Club would share the Stadium with the London Irish Rugby Union Club and, in addition, it has seen many special events including major internationals and concerts.

The following photograph shows the Madejski Stadium football ground in 2010.

The Club's biggest impact on Southern Reading, along with the rest of the town and indeed the wider community in Berkshire and beyond, came from its rise into the Premier League in 2006 after winning the Championship with the highest points ever achieved in that Division by any Club. There was tremendous excitement for the town and the club's place in the top League was maintained for two years before dropping back into the Championship in 2008.

A sustained spell in the top flight would have given a large boost to hotels, restaurants and others in the entertainment and associated industries. At the same time, of course, it would have put an increased strain on the already congested roads, particularly around the Stadium area. This immediately would have put pressure on the Junction 11 rebuild timetable but that was completed in 2010. Plans were put on hold with the Council for an enlargement of the stand area to increase capacity from 24,000 to 38,000, in readiness for any future leap back into the Premier League, which finally took place in 2012 after the club won the Championship title for the second time and ownership changed. However, another relegation back to the Championship at the end of that 2012/2013 season meant that only time would tell whether the Club would make a quick return and a longer stay next time giving the Club the assurance to carry out the enlargement work.

The photograph below shows a Reading Bus painted to celebrate the promotion to the Premier League in 2006.

During the summer of 2014, the Club finally resolved its difficulties with ownership having, for that short period, been jointly owned by Sir John Madejski and the Russian investor, Anton Zingarevich, with Sir John remaining as Chairman. The solution was found when a Thai consortium bought the whole of the Club in 2014 with Sir John being retained as co-Chairman. The Thai owners took a step further when they announced plans for development of part of the car park adjoining the Stadium for the possible erection of a conference centre. The Football Club was still chasing promotion to the Premier League at the end of 2016. New Chinese owners took over a majority share in the Club and stadium from the Thais in Spring 2017 after clearance from the Football authorities. The club reached the Championship play-off final at Wembley in May 2017 but lost out on penalties.

Sir John Madejski

Born in Stoke-on-Trent in 1941, John Madejski moved to Reading with his parents at the age of 13 and lived in Wokingham Road, from which he attended Alfred Sutton School (now the Primary School). He made his fortune as an entrepreneur in publishing, starting with the periodical Thames Valley Trader in 1976, which evolved into the Auto Trader. He sold off his Hurst Publishing Company in 1998 for a reported £174m. In recent years he has become Reading's most well-known philanthropist as well as businessman.

His most significant personal achievement was the transformation of the Reading Football Club after taking over as Chairman in 1990, building them a new stadium (the Madejski Stadium), which opened for the club's use in 1998, and then leading them into the Premier League for the first time in the club's history in 2006. Another well-known achievement has been his contribution to the transformation of the old Ashmead School into a new, thriving City Academy which was called the John Madejski Academy and opened in 2006. Among his lesser known contributions to the town have been funding of a department at Reading University's Henley Business School, the funding of an Art Gallery at the Town Hall, and a donation to a lecture theatre at the University. He is also a benefactor to the Royal Academy of Arts.

His business contributions to the town's development include the proposal for a new project to rebuild the Station Hill complex, for which plans were in discussion with the Government from 2008 and building started in 2015.

John Madejski can be seen in 2006 with members of the Reading FC team at the front of the parading bus, which is passing along Whitley Street.

In 2008, he was installed as Chancellor of Reading University (from which he announced that he would retire at the end of 2016) after being made an honorary Doctor of Letters and, in the 2009 New Year's honours, he was knighted. He is also a Freeman of the Borough of Reading and a Deputy Lieutenant of Berkshire. In 2015 he was awarded a Lifetime Achievement Award at the European Business Awards.

Speedway and Greyhound Racing and Casinos

The old Reading Greyhound and Speedway Stadium in West Reading was closed in 1975 and these sports moved to a new stadium on a former rubbish tip on Council land at Smallmead beyond the end of Bennet Road well before the A33 Relief Road was built. The Smallmead Greyhound and Speedway Stadium was developed by Reg Fearman, a speedway promoter, and his investor colleagues who built the arena and stands from scratch in less than a year – see the stadium under construction in the photograph below.

It opened in April 1975 with a seating capacity of 1500 and total capacity of some 15000. The greyhound track ran round the outside of the speedway track. Access to the Stadium was along a dirt track road via Bennet Road and past the replacement Civic Amenity site. Near the pits, there was an unmade car park which was often covered in shale from the races (as were the cars!). The event was in two parts, the first being the main meeting with 13 races between Reading Racers and the visiting team and then there was a break for refreshments before the second half which was normally for junior riders.

Reading Racers became a very successful and popular speedway team during the 1970s and 1980s in the top UK league, producing some of the top racers in the country. Memorable stars of the Racers' team in those early years included Anders Michanek, Per Jonsson, Dave Jessup and Bernie Leigh. Under Dave Lanning, the Racers topped the Premier League in 1981. Later the team went off the boil and this led to a re-launch as the Reading Bulldogs in 2006.

The immediate effect seemed to be very rewarding as they flew high in the Elite League. However, in October 2008, the then owners of the Stadium decided that it was time for a new stadium for both sports as the land was required for redevelopment. The Reading Racers (they had reinstated their original name) had to hold their last ever meeting at Smallmead after 40 years of Speedway in the town and the greyhound racing, which had also been very popular, ended after 33 years at the Smallmead Stadium.

At the time that the stadium closed, there was still the expectation that both sports would be able to restart at a new 'Racino', offering a Speedway and Greyhound Stadium coupled with a Casino, on land near Island Road together with a shuttle bus service into the town centre, after planning approval was given to Stadia UK in 2007. Approval was renewed in 2011 with a 3-year extension. Stadia UK finally gave up on the project in 2012 after casino companies pulled out. This left the Speedway and Greyhound Racing with nowhere to go in the foreseeable future despite an attempt in 2013 to persuade the Council to help fund the project possibly on a different site nearby. Nevertheless, Reading Racers was revived in 2016, albeit without a stadium, to compete in races at Eastbourne's track.

Eventually, a brand new casino was built in Rose Kiln Lane and opened as the Grosvenor G Casino in March 2013, thus thwarting the plans of the Racino project developers. The £6.4m venture, operated by the Grosvenor Casino group, provided a Lady G Show Bar, restaurant and modern bar, together with games and sport lounges and a number of conference rooms.

Public Houses

As was indicated earlier in this chapter, there were many public houses in the Whitley area (dating back in some cases hundreds of years), notably The King's Head at the south end of Whitley Street, the Queen's Head in Christchurch Road and the Four Horseshoes together with The World Turned Upside Down and The Grenadier all in Basingstoke Road. There were the Merry Maidens and the Sportsman in Shinfield Road. Later additions were the Northumberland Arms (shortened later to The Northumberland), the Carousel and the Whitley Tavern in Northumberland Avenue together with the Engineers' Arms at the junction of Whitley Wood Road and Whitley Wood Lane.

However, the demise of public houses was quite widespread in Whitley over the late 20th and early 21st centuries. This happened, for example, to the Engineers' Arms and also The Whitley Tavern, on the corner of Northumberland Avenue and Hartland Road. The Engineers' Arms was closed and later demolished in 2007 for a housing development and replaced with a block of flats named 'Engineers Court'. The Whitley Tavern was closed in 2006 and put up for sale at £0.6m in 2009, after a planning application for development was turned down; it was still boarded up a year later and was finally demolished in 2011 and replaced with a block of flats. The Carousel on the junction of Long Barn Lane and Northumberland Avenue had already been demolished and replaced with flats some years previously. For similar reasons, the permanent closure, after a few years of uncertainty, of The Northumberland took place in 2009 and this was sold the following year for conversion into a local supermarket.

This resulted in there being no remaining public houses in Central Whitley at all and only a few on the periphery (The Queen's Head, The Sportsman, for example), while places such as the Four Horseshoes, the World Turned Upside Down (see the photograph below taken about 1980) and the Merry Maidens became better known for food in various ways.

The Four Horseshoes, an old coaching inn, dated back to the 18th century at least, and it is understood to have been known sometime in the 19th century as The Long Barn. It was completely rebuilt around 1950 as a large public house. Around 1990, restaurant facilities were added. Later in the 1990s, it was converted into the Mongolian Barbecue restaurant and afterwards was renamed the Eastern Pearl restaurant. However, it was put up for sale around 2012 and, in 2016, it was demolished. Recently plans have been largely agreed by the Council for two apartment blocks to be built on the site to accommodate a total of 34 single rooms for students with provision for amenity space.

Meanwhile the World Turned Upside Down was taken over around 1980 and became a Harvester restaurant with a Travelodge facility added soon after and this continues to be a popular venue as a Crown Carverie and Travelodge.

The Merry Maidens started life in the 19th century as the Maidens and it was named after a circle of stones in Cornwall used by the Druids, where the legend says that the maidens had been turned to stone for dancing on a Sunday. For this reason, the inn had four stone maidens lined along the front – these can be seen on the photograph below which was taken about 1905 and shows the local hunt and supporters gathered outside. It was completely renovated in the early/mid-20th century and its name was shortened again to The Maidens in the early 2000s. The inn was sold and converted to a 'Sainsbury's local' supermarket outlet in 2014.

The Grenadier Inn in Whitley Wood (Basingstoke Road) had started as a beer house in the 1840s and later became a public house, which had two tall model Grenadier Guards standing either side of the entrance. It was demolished and re-built as the Post House Hotel at the time that the M4 was being built and then was converted into the present Holiday Inn as the commercial development of West Whitley took place.

There has been one new addition in the Whitley area in recent times and that was the opening of The Trooper Potts pub-restaurant at 350, Basingstoke Road next door to Aldi's in 2015/16. This was named after Trooper Fred Potts, the Katesgrove soldier who was awarded the Victoria Cross during the Great War for his valour during the battle at Gallipoli in 1915. That was where he saved the life of his comrade Trooper Arthur Andrews, who was badly injured, by dragging him to safety on a shovel.

The Savoy Cinema

This was known locally as the 'Cabbage' (because of its name!) and was very popular with Whitley people, particularly during the Second World War when it was an opportunity for servicemen to go and relax and be entertained while home on leave. It had opened in 1936 during the period of the explosion of cinemas across the country, in particular in the residential areas. The cinema was also much loved by the local children for Saturday morning pictures with cartoons and other films which they could watch and enjoy with their friends. It finally closed in 1961, having lost the interest of the local people primarily because of the impact of television and the easy access to the larger cinemas in the town centre.

The following photograph was taken at the time the Savoy cinema was being built in 1936.

Whitley Arts Festival

A South Reading event, which started in a small way in 2004 and has become something of a major annual fixture in the town, has been the Whitley Arts Festival, which is held at several venues particularly in and around Whitley during the autumn with the main focus at the South Reading Youth and Community Centre. This festival has given many local people the opportunity to show off their talents in the interests of developing the Whitley community and includes many workshops and performances across the arts spectrum (dance, drama, painting and poetry). The festival has become well-known across Reading and beyond the town.

Churches' Fun Day

Another event that has become an annual fixture in Whitley has been the South Reading Churches' Fun Day. This is a community event at Rabson's Recreation Ground, which is organised by the Whitley Group of Churches of various denominations. It has been held every summer since 2004 and regularly attracts thousands of people.

Reading Half Marathon

Since 1983, the Reading Half Marathon has been a major event in the town. Originally it was started and finished at the University's Whiteknights campus after making a circuit through Whitley and the town centre. The first running of the Half-Marathon attracted some 5000 participants. It is now much bigger (some 15000 or more started in 2016) and in recent years it has been run from Green Park, still going around Whitley, the University campus and the town centre before ending with a grand finish around the inside of the Madejski Stadium to loud cheering from the crowds of spectators.

The photograph on the next page shows the Half Marathon runners on Christchurch Road in 2010 as they approach to turn into the top of Kendrick Road.

PART 2

Memories of Whitley Life in Times Past

This part is devoted to the recollections of family and friends that have lived in Whitley for some of the last eighty years and more. What has particularly been apparent in collecting these memories from the kind people who gave them to me has been their willingness to talk about their early lives, the environment in which they grew up and how that has impacted on them. I am most grateful to them for sharing their thoughts with me and giving us an insight into how Whitley is remembered in the early to mid-20th century.

It starts with my own early memories of Whitley Wood when I arrived in Reading in the early 1960s......

"When I moved with my family to Reading from Tadley as a teenager in 1961, our new house was in Alandale Close, off Whitley Wood Road. My Dad was a telephone engineer with the GPO at the time (now, of course, it is BT) and had been responsible for the AWRE Aldermaston telephone system. We moved to Reading because he had a new job in the town. Our house faced down the Close and looked across to the RAF Training Camp. The Camp had a large wire mesh fence surrounding the staff quarters in Anson Crescent though that fence has long since gone along with the Camp. On one side of the Camp, towards Whitley Wood Lane, was the Shirley Avenue and Woodside Way estate, which included many prefabricated houses from before the War, and those were replaced with modern housing in the 1960s. On the other side, towards Shinfield Road, was the Winton Road estate on the side of the hill with smaller roads coming off of that main road. Most of Central Whitley was developed into housing estates by then, only small developments coming afterwards.

"There were shops towards the bottom of Northumberland Avenue on the right hand side adjoining Whitley Wood Road. On the opposite side of the road was the terminus for the No. 15 Northumberland Avenue trolley bus from the town centre and, today, it is the No. 5 Emerald bus.

"The shops included Lambeth's newsagents (originally Maynard's), where I worked as a young paper boy. These days very few people have their papers delivered - they collect them from the shop or get their news on-line or from the television and so paper boys are largely a thing of the past. I was delivering papers along Whitley Wood Road from Northumberland Avenue to Hartland Road including Alandale Close, Wentworth Avenue and up the steep hill of Winton Road (not so much fun in the winter when the roads were icy – I came off my bike more than once!). Around the corner in Whitley Wood Road was another newsagent, Forbuoys.

"Close to Lambeth's, there was also J R Butler Chemists, where I worked on Saturdays and in school holidays when I was 16. While there, I used to help the pharmacist dispense the medicines and also assist with keeping the shelves stacked in the shop.

"While my younger brothers went to Geoffrey Field Junior School, I travelled by bus through the town to Stoneham Grammar School in Tilehurst. The Head Master was Dr Sidney Smith. There I made new friends and particularly enjoyed playing in the school orchestra. On my way home, the bus journey gave me the chance to spend time in the town with my friends, listening to records in our favourite music shops (Browns, Hickies and Rumbelows) and stopping in a coffee bar, before going home for tea.

"In my spare time I went to St Paul's Church Hall for youth club activities, particularly playing table tennis and listening to the latest records. Later the Church Hall was turned into cottages. For evening refreshment, we all went off to the Cordingley family's fish and chip shop, the Yorkshire Fisheries, just round the corner in Basingstoke Road. I attended St Paul's Church in Whitley Wood Lane and sang in the boys' choir. I was confirmed at Christ Church in, I think, 1962. Next door to St Paul's Church lived the local bobby, Sergeant Bill Amor, with his family and further down Whitley Wood Lane was Darvall's coal merchants who delivered coal and coke products around the local area. Further along, at the junction with Whitley Wood Road, was the Engineers' Arms public house, by the roundabout which was the terminus of the No.16 Whitley Wood trolley bus. It is still the route for that service from the town centre, though now it is an Emerald bus service, the No. 6, and extended a bit further in Whitley Wood. I used to cycle to Buckland Road to Fred Lester's barber's shop to get my hair cut.

"On summer days it was pleasant to walk or cycle out through the fields of Little Lea Farm near to the west of Basingstoke Road in Whitley Wood. That area was largely undeveloped with just the Grenadier public house, the Whitley Park recreation ground and the farms. Of course, in those days, there was no M4 or Junction 11, no Shire Hall and Basingstoke Road was unbroken from Whitley through to Three Mile Cross, Spencers Wood and beyond. Also Shinfield Road was continuous from Shinfield Green to the Black Boy public house and on to Shinfield village and Arborfield village. Whitley Wood Lane was much shorter and extended only as a lane from the Engineer's Arms past Margaret Close.

"Later on, Digital Computers bought land in Basingstoke Road opposite the old

Church Hall and The Grenadier was demolished and replaced with a brand new Post House Hotel as the M4 was being opened up a bit further south. Further towards the town in Basingstoke Road on the river side of the road were the Little Miss Muffet Junket factory and the Gillette factory (a landmark building then as it still is today with its distinctive frontage) along with various other factories, warehouses and businesses.

"I lived in Whitley Wood for three years before the family moved again, near to Burghfield Road in Southcote, at the time that I had just left school. I had started working at GPO Telephones in Reading and then moved to work on mobile radio systems in 1971 in London, where I stayed for more than thirty years, continuing to work for Post Office Telephones, which became British Telecom in the early 1980s.

"A few years after leaving Whitley Wood, I was back again in Whitley but this time as a married man with a son, living at the top of Northumberland Avenue – on the hill."

Barbara

Barbara and her two older brothers (Tony and Melvyn), older sister (Irene, known as Joan) and younger brother (Brian) moved with their parents back to Whitley in 1950 into a house at the bottom end of Northumberland Avenue near to Hartland Road…..

"I was born in Brixham Road and, after a short stay in Tilehurst where Brian was born, the family moved to Northumberland Avenue. Geoff and Sue were born there and on hand to assist as necessary was the local midwife, Nurse Trotter, who lived in Hartland Road. Mum loved this area as it was close to the shops and the bus stops. It was there that each of us stayed until we flew the nest.

"After the move, I started going to Blagdon Road Nursery. I remember having to lie down to go to sleep after lunch but, really, I would have preferred to carry on playing with the toys! When I was five years old, I went on to Whitley Park Infants School as my older sister Joan was already at the Juniors. My abiding memory of that school is the smell of warm milk, which we were given at playtime in the morning in small bottles, and of the ink in the inkwells on desks, both of which I didn't like and the smells have stayed with me to this day! Joan moved on to Wilson School the following year and Mum moved me to Geoffrey Field Infants School, which was much nearer. I met another little girl there, called Roslyn, and we remained firm friends throughout our school years together.

"When we first moved to Northumberland Avenue, there were fields on the opposite side of the road where gipsies camped their caravans and tethered their horses to wooden posts. Also on that side of the road was a rambling cottage – known as Eddystone cottage – which was very overgrown and had a large orchard of fruit trees in a long back garden. I was often sent to buy some apples and plums, which Mrs Hawkes, the old lady who lived there, weighed out on some large scales with metal weights. Behind the orchard, there was a big field and my sister, Joan, used to go and play with two children of similar age to her that were often at the cottage. In the front garden, I remember a large model of a lighthouse, which was a local landmark. I was given a new bicycle for Christmas which came from Smith's cycle shop at the end of Whitley Wood Road. I was often sent on errands for Mum, riding proudly on my new bike, and I also rode it to and from school.

"I went with Mum to see Dr Vann at his surgery in his house in Basingstoke Road on several occasions. Because there was no appointment system like surgeries today, there was sometimes a queue through his hallway and down his front garden path but the doctor made sure that he saw everyone that had queued each day. On our way back home from there, we might go in the Post Office nearby or on to the shops nearer Buckland Road. There was the chemist's shop with Hadley's hairdressers over the top. Next door was Broadhurst's second-hand furniture shop. Joan remembers that there was an alleyway at the side of Broadhurst's, where coal was sold. Sometimes she carried an accumulator for the radio from Brixham Road to that alleyway to exchange it for a charged one. On the corner opposite the Savoy Cinema was Rooney's newsagent's shop where Mum belonged to the Christmas Club so that she could save for the favourite annuals we had chosen.

"We continued walking along Buckland Road and round into Northumberland Avenue until we reached the bakers where Mum bought a crusty loaf and also, occasionally as a treat, she bought us two fresh cream meringues and these would be placed in a small box rather than a paper bag to avoid crushing them. Then there was Tom the butcher's where Mum would give him her order, which he would weigh out and wrap up, after which he would add up the total and call it to a lady cashier in a little wooden cubicle where you went to pay the bill. Further along there was a lovely fish and chip shop where families bought their Friday night supper. We passed the Community Centre and went on past the Welfare Clinic. That was where young babies were checked and weighed and the mother would collect tins of dried milk, orange juice and cod liver oil - as we grew older and went to school, we were immunised against various infectious diseases there and also saw the school dentist. I walked on down Northumberland Avenue chatting to Mum, with young Geoff or Sue in their 'Tansad' pushchair, until we reached home. Those were some of the happy times I enjoyed as a child.

"Joan has told me that Hadley's hairdresser's was where she once went, after her day at school, to have her hair permed as a birthday treat from Mum. It involved electric perm rods being put into her hair, connected by wires to a hood. When the rods were taken out, her hair was extremely frizzy, which she didn't like at all. The next day she had to go to school and, at the end of lessons for the day, she was called to one side and the teacher enquired, "Irene, what has happened to your hair, can you calm it down by tomorrow? You can't wear your beret properly and your hair is hiding the school badge on it!"

"On one occasion, when I had been to see Dr Vann with Mum, we were stopped by the school beadle who wanted to know why the little girl was not at school. Mum explained that I had been to see the doctor. When the beadle was satisfied, he thanked Mum and went on his way. The beadle could often be seen riding on his bike round the streets looking out for children who were not at school.

"I remember a man with a horse and cart who used to bring fruit and vegetables around the streets to sell to the local people - his name was Mr Appleby. There was also a muffin man who used to walk round the street, an ice cream man with a motorcycle and side car and a rag-and-bone man with a horse and cart.

"Further down from our house towards Whitley Wood Road was a hardware shop, called Richard's, where I bought a dinner service with matching casseroles for my 'bottom drawer' – it was white Pyrex with a pattern on it, which was very popular in those days.

"After Geoffrey Field Juniors, I moved on to George Palmer Senior Girls' School at the top of Northumberland Avenue. During my time there, I remember going to the Whitley Community Centre for some of my lessons and the classes were under the name of 'Cintra'. When I was there for classes, Mum was sometimes doing some shopping and happened to walk past during playtime and she might pass through the wire fence some sweets for me to eat.

"The following year, in 1960, the new Girls' School, Southlands, opened after Easter and we were told to pick up our chairs and take them down the Avenue from George Palmer to Southlands. I continued at Southlands until I left at the end of the following school year.

"Later, when I was working at Gillette's in my late teens, I often used to walk along to see Dad during my lunch break as he was working at Crittall Metal Windows factory in Basingstoke Road which was further down past Bennet Road. We would have a chat and then I returned to work for the afternoon.

"I went with my friend, Roslyn, to the Court School of Dancing in Duke Street to learn to dance while we were still at school. Then, having left school and, being a teenager, I went out in the evening with my friends in my pencil skirt, high heels and beehive hair style (made popular in this country at that time by Dusty Springfield). I can remember pencil skirts being very fashionable but they didn't make it easy for me to get on and off buses when I was going dancing at the Majestic ballroom in Caversham Road! We enjoyed the dancing and seeing the resident band, led by Ted or George Watkins, with their singer Tony on a Saturday night. Sometimes we went to the Olympia ballroom in London Street to see some of the top groups of the time which often appeared there, including Acker Bilk's Jazz Band whose record of 'Stranger on the Shore' I had just bought. Then, when I later married at Christ Church, I moved away from my parents' home and started my new life."

Melvyn

Melvyn was born in Brixham Road during the war. He had an older brother and sister (Tony and Joan)......

"At the time that I was born, my father was a corporal with the Royal Gloucesters. He was eventually promoted to Warrant Officer with them. When at home, I recall my Dad treated me and my siblings like his own little army. Like many families during the war, Dad kept a vegetable plot and rabbits in the back garden.

"My best friend Brian Wicks, whom I call BJ, lived in the same road and his Dad always seemed to have a more interesting job than mine – BJ's Dad was a Leading Aircraftsman with the RAF during the war and then went to work at Venners, whilst volunteering as a Special Constable.

"One of my early memories was standing on the back door step of Brixham Road watching the search lights, which I was told was situated on the Hartland Road roundabout, and I could occasionally hear the firing of the Anti-Aircraft gun.

"Then the family moved away to Tilehurst, where we stayed for a short time. I remember that the house had no electricity, only gas for lighting and heating and we had to go up some steps to the front door. Our family then moved to Northumberland Avenue where we had electricity if you put pennies or shillings in the meter. As a result of the size of Whitley estate, there was always a shortage of shillings so one of my jobs was to go to the bus terminus, where the Northumberland Avenue trolley buses turned round, to ask the conductor for change. The terminus was opposite the lighthouse cottage. The road from the town was made up with tarmac to that point, the rest being a dirt lane, even though houses had been built to the corner with Whitley Wood Road. Later, once the road had been completely made up, the terminus was moved to that bottom corner of the Avenue, where it remains to this day.

"I attended Whitley Park Nursery School, which was opposite where we lived in Brixham Road, so that Mum could go to work in the gas mask factory in the Basingstoke Road area. I recall my gas mask had Mickey Mouse ears. I then moved up to Whitley Park Junior School where Mr Capel was the headmaster and Mr Fox, who always wore a brown house coat and pushed a wheel barrow, was the school caretaker whilst Mr Chalk looked after the school grounds. I recall the school being flooded out when someone turned the fire hydrants on and the police came to our house to make enquiries. As the police were at the front door, my brother slipped out of the back at break-neck speed!

"Due to overcrowding, I transferred to Geoffrey Field Junior School when it opened in 1951. Mr Payton was the headmaster. Although my family couldn't afford school uniform, I was made milk monitor and I gave my friends the warmed bottles and those that annoyed me the cold bottles of milk. I had the perfect attendance at Junior School and was presented a book but far more important to me was the daily school dinner!

"Like my sister Barbara, I recall seeing gipsies camped on the land opposite our house when we first moved in to Northumberland Avenue. Being not long after the war, there were still old war-time army Nissen huts and prefabricated houses near our home. Close to our house was a roundabout; on the other side of it, to right and left, were these pre-fabricated houses. The Nissen huts were further along, where the Ashmead School buildings were erected a few years later. I remember going into a Nissen hut one day with my older sister, Joan, to see a friend and was surprised to find that there was no flooring in it, just grass growing there! However, the huts were quite well laid out with pot-bellied boilers at each end.

"Sometimes I had to go with my older brother, Tony, to Darvall's coal merchants in Whitley Wood Lane after school to bring back a sack of coal in a pushchair when it was needed. Part of the journey was along a dirt track road and it was very difficult to move the pushchair along without tipping it. However, because it tended to be later in the day that we went, there was often a queue and, as a result, the merchant's supplies ran out - we had to go home without our hundredweight of coal and the house might be cold that night until we could go again the next day!

"As a young boy without any money, I remember spending many hours wandering round the area until it was time to return home for tea. You couldn't have that sort of freedom today as a child but it was very common in those days! As youngsters, we made our own entertainment - we went scrumping apples from the lighthouse garden. The lighthouse was in the garden of the rambling cottage across the road from where we lived - it was a large model painted white. It could be lit up but was kept dark after the Second World War started. I used to visit the old lady as well and, on one occasion, after going through the five-bar gate into the garden, I was allowed to see the lighthouse alight but that was very rare as it had been largely unlit since before the War. There was also a younger woman there; she may have been living in the other Eddystone cottage next door, which was demolished when the Catholic Church was built in the late 1950s.

"Other free or enterprising activities of mine around that time included swimming at Monkey Island on the river Kennet and collecting beer bottles and taking them to the Bottle and Jug entrance of the World Turned Upside Down. Sometimes when the bar staff were busy or not very attentive, we nicked some of the bottles back and got another tuppence each for them.

"On the Basingstoke Road was Nicholls' Pickles, a small family-run enterprise. This was in a previously detached house, painted in a dull yellow, and this was another source of income for me. In exchange for suitable jam jars or preferred larger vessels for the pickling products, we would be given a few pence. One of my memories whilst at Ashmead School was that a teacher, Mr Owen, wrote an article for 'The Torch', the annual school publication, describing cycling from his home to the school along Elgar Road during which he could enjoy the waft of the produce from Nicholls' Pickles.

"From about the age of 8, the Savoy Cinema, which was next door to Nicholls' Pickles on the Basingstoke Road, became as familiar to me as my own home. The emergency exit was towards the toilets at the back of the building and opened out into Buckland Road. When a friend went into the cinema with one of their parents, he would head for the toilets and open the fire door so that I and about a dozen others could sneak in. There were 2 floors but I don't remember ever going upstairs where one could purchase something to eat. I watched anything current at the time, mostly black and white films produced by Ealing Studios & The Rank Organisation including A Town Like Alice, The Bridge Over the River Kwai and Lawrence of Arabia.

"In Basingstoke Road was Gillette's factory. Gillette's was previously a Bourjois factory that sold perfume, in particular a very popular one at the time called 'Evening in Paris', and other beauty products. I recall seeing the famous clock tower on the main frontage being marked with the letters of the company name (BOURJOIS) from the clock downwards on the tower. In nearby Bennet Road, many Reading Corporation trolley buses could be seen where they were stored, these buses being used on all the main routes in Reading and regularly seen on the routes in Whitley.

"As time went by during the 1950s, the family saw the Ashmead School built and the Christ the King Church built, both close by where we lived. Later, in the

1960s, the Whitley Tavern public house was built on the corner of Northumberland Avenue and Hartland Road near our home.

"From Geoffrey Field Junior School, I went on to Ashmead School from 1953, the year after it opened. After I left the School, I started work and went on to join the RAF. In the meantime, my older brother, Tony, had already joined the Navy."

Patricia

Patricia has always lived near the boundary of Whitley, at the top of Basingstoke Road on Whitley Hill, both through her early life in Weymouth Terrace and Derby Cottages and then on to her married life………

"The Whitley that I remember from my childhood is very different to the one we see today. I was born in the 1940s and at first lived with my Mum, Dad and grandparents on the Basingstoke Road in one of the terrace houses near to Whitley Street. Later we moved into a semi-detached house next door to my grandparents and this is where I spent the rest of my childhood and teenage years.

"All the houses in those days had a front garden with a gate and railings or a wall and only those with a driveway would park their cars at the front of the house. There were no signs of the large plastic wheelie bins that fill the front gardens today. Any vegetable waste that we had back then would be tipped into the pig bin which was outside on the road.

"While the back gardens in the terrace houses provided space for some of our flowers and vegetables to be grown, many local men would also take on an allotment and my father was no different. His first plot was at the end of Newcastle Road, which is now housing, but this was a fair distance for us to walk to as we didn't have a car. As soon as a plot became available on land at the bottom of Swainstone Road, he moved there which meant it was far more accessible.

"We never had central heating so, just before winter set in, the chimney sweep would call and I would go and wait outside to see the brushes pop out of the top of the chimney. It was a common sight in those days but just a distant memory now.

"On Christmas morning the Salvation Army or the Spring Gardens Band would march along the Basingstoke Road, stopping at various points to play carols. My parents would go outside and put a donation into their collecting box.

"In 1953 the local community celebrated the Queen's coronation with a street party. I was very young but I believe our local one was in Swainstone Road and as a souvenir of the occasion I was given a commemorative spoon to keep. We were very lucky to have a television so my grandparents invited our neighbour in to watch the Coronation Service with us.

"I can recall seeing the coalman delivering the coal in large bags. He would carry them on his back and then tip them into the shed in the rear garden. It would sound like thunder rumbling every time he tipped another bag.

"We used to have our milk from the Co-op who my grandfather worked for as a delivery man. As a special treat I would occasionally be allowed to go with him and his faithful horse Nobby on their round in the Addington Road area.

"Trolley-buses served the local area and I remember often watching them stopping because the poles had come off the overhead wire. The conductor would have to go and hook them back on again using a very long retriever pole which was slid back under the bus when it was ready to go again.

"During the 1950s and 60s, Smith's Coaches was the local coach company. At about 8.30 am on Saturday mornings they passed by my house as they made their way south on day trips and holidays. We always went with Smith's on our annual holiday to the Isle of Wight or Weymouth. The pick-up point was in Mill Lane where a long line of coaches would be waiting with the drivers ticking our names off their passenger lists. On the way home they would often drop us at Whitley Chapel which meant it was only a short walk back to our house.

"School plays a large part in everyone's life and, when I reached school age, I started at George Palmer School before later moving on to Katesgrove Secondary and Cintra Secondary School.

"I still have my old school reports and the first GPJ (George Palmer Junior) magazine. This magazine was a collection of contributions from those of us who were pupils in July 1957 and included crosswords, poems, articles about trips out and the results of the school football and netball teams against other local schools such as Geoffrey Field, Southcote and Katesgrove. It also states that 'the uniform is navy tunics, white blouses, red ties and navy blue cardigans. There are approximately 500 children on the roll'.

"One of my most vivid memories is towards the end of my school days when we had to model our latest needlework creations in a fashion show. I wore a blue dress which I designed myself and called an every-day summer dress. According to my notes in my old school book, I thought that the best material to use would be a washing cotton because 'it can be washed out easily and will always come up clean therefore I do not have to worry if it gets dirty'.

"On Saturday morning during the late 1950s, I used to take piano lessons from a lady who lived in Lincoln Road. Sadly, I have forgotten much of what I learnt back then and would probably struggle to string the notes together today.

"My first job after leaving school was working in Milwards in Broad Street. While there I remember I bought myself a pair of very trendy white leather boots with a large leather bow on them. I wish I had kept them as they have now become a collectable fashion item of the 1960s. After leaving Milwards, I moved to the opposite end of the retail sector by working at the offices of Hallmark Cards in Cradock Road.

"By the mid-1960s, I was regularly attending the Court School of Dancing along with a group of friends from work. This was in Duke Street opposite the Ship Hotel so I could easily get there from home. It was during this time that I met my husband Colin. We married in 1970 at Christ Church and four years later our daughter Caroline was born.

"During my life in Whitley I've seen many shops at Whitley Street come and go. Some of the older ones I remember are:

The Co-op; Potter's Barbers; Miss Bance's sweet shop; The haberdashery/drapery shop; The Chocolate Box; Jelly's Stores; Whitby's Cameras; Eighteen & Cox butchers and fishmongers; Home & Colonial grocery; Merritt's bicycles.

"In 1988, the top end of Basingstoke Road was closed for four months while the old Victorian sewage system and utility pipework was all replaced. This meant that we (the residents) had to drive around the manhole covers and holes in the road to get to our homes. Just walking to the local newsagents was sometimes like taking on an obstacle course as we worked our way around workmen, equipment, uneven ground, holes and sometimes burst water mains which would spurt the water into the air like a fountain!

"Most recently, I took a photograph of the 2012 Olympic torch relay as it entered Christchurch Gardens from Basingstoke Road. I know that when Britain last hosted the Olympics in 1948 the torch was also carried through this part of Whitley as my parents had taken a photograph at the time on the same corner. Back then, I doubt it would have arrived with quite so much commercial sponsorship at the head of the procession yet I am sure the excitement and enthusiasm from the local community was much the same.

"Over the decades I've seen many changes in the part of Whitley that I call home and I'm sure there will be many more to come in the future".

Peggy

Peggy says that, after she was born, her first home was in Alpine Street at her grandparents' house. She lived with her parents, Gladys and Stanley, and her older brothers, Denis and Stanley, who was known to the family as Maurice to save confusion with his Dad……

"A while after I was born, we moved to our own home in Linden Road and started a family life there. At that time, Maurice started at Redlands Infants School and Den at Redlands Junior School. Mum walked them from home along Shinfield Road to get them to and from school, with me in a pushchair, and that was quite a distance for them to walk.

"I was one of the first children to start at Ridgeway Infants School at the age of five in 1929, just after it had opened. My brothers continued to go to Redlands to save interrupting their education by moving them to Ridgeway. In due course, both my brothers moved on to the Redlands Senior School.

"I remember that our back garden had a gate at the end, which opened into an alleyway leading to a park at the back of the houses where we children could play. It had swings and slides together with plenty of space to play games. I sometimes went there with my young friends to play but, being a bit of a 'tomboy', I preferred to go over the road from the front of the house to play in the woods with the boys, climbing trees, scrumping apples and generally having fun.

"By the time I had finished at Junior School in 1935, Mum had had two more children, Ken and Mary. I went to join my brother Maurice at Redlands Senior School, Den having already left by then. At secondary school, I showed great promise at sports, especially gymnastics in the school gym and athletics at Palmer Park. Dad used to cycle from where he worked at the Berkshire Printing Company in Oxford Road after he had finished for the day so that he could cheer me on when I took part in the athletics competitions. I remember that I was often being called out from lessons to go to the gym and demonstrate to other children the right way to perform a vault over a horse or other exercises. I was particularly strong at athletics and became long jump champion at Berkshire schools' level, also competing in the relay races, and winning many medals. I went on to participate in the all-England schools competitions, training at the Berkshire schools' training ground near Maidenhead.

"At 14, I left Redlands Senior School and started at Heelas department store in the town, giving up my sporting activities. My first job was to work at the cash desk in various departments (haberdashery, gowns, etc.) and then I progressed to invoicing before moving into the Accounts Department.

"By 1942, when I was 18, I remember that my friend and I decided to join the Women's Land Army as part of the War effort, my two older brothers already being in the Navy, one with the Russian Convoy, the other in the Mediterranean. Mum was very upset about me wanting to join up as well but she went with me to the enrolment office near Forbury Gardens, where I was signed up.

"Dad, who had served in the Army in the Great War, was working at the Printing Company by day and had joined the local Home Guard unit. He was assigned to fire watch duty at night in the tower at Christ Church.

"After being signed up to the Land Army, my friend and I were first sent to a hostel at Winkfield and, suitably attired for the work, helped on local farms. The first task we were given was picking tomatoes. Then we moved on to a hostel at Brimpton, near the Colthrop Mills and Greenham Common, and there we worked as part of a team that went round local farms with a threshing machine to reap the harvest and collect the large bags of corn. It was heavy work but we soon became used to it. Some Italian prisoners-of-war were despatched to help us with our work and I had to assign them to individual tasks on the farms. The Italians were very hard workers.

"Being close to the American air base at Greenham Common, I remember GIs coming in a truck to pick up the Land Army girls and take us back to the base so that we could join in the dances put on by them from time to time. We enjoyed ourselves very much and had a really good time. Chocolate and cigarettes were given to us by the GIs – but I don't remember any nylons!

"Each weekend I was able to go home to Linden Road, with my friend, and we used to thumb a lift from Brimpton to get there and back. My favourite Saturday night out was to go roller-skating at the rink in Palmer Hall in West Street. It was there at Palmer Hall that I met my future husband, Stan, who was serving in the Navy.

"When he was on leave, Stan often used to walk me home after we had been out for the evening and we would stand at the front gate to say goodnight. After a short while, my Mum would open the front door to put out some milk bottles, rattling them as she did so. Then, after a bit longer, she would come out again with some more milk bottles, rattling them again. I remember that I couldn't make out where all these milk bottles had come from - I could only imagine that Mum was rattling the same ones again to let us both know that we had been at the gate long enough!

"At the end of the War, when I was 21, both Stan and I were able to go back to normal civilian life. My job was at the War Agricultural Office near the Forbury until we were married at Christ Church the following year. The same year that we were married also saw my two older brothers, Denis and Maurice, married at Christ Church.

"Stan and I started our married life together living in Newtown with my aunt and uncle, Ivy and Charlie, before moving to what became our own family home in Tilehurst where we brought up our two children, Alan and Mary Ann. I never lost my love for sport and used to go to football with Stan and Alan and still enjoy the main sporting events on the television.

"Over time, the family home at Linden Road saw much association with the Navy. My three brothers had been sailors and my younger sister, Mary, and I both had married sailors.

"I have fond memories of my parents' home in Linden Road where we all got together at family gatherings and the married children would come to them with the grandchildren. It was a chance for all of us to catch up with each other. We also organised coach trips to the seaside from time to time, taking some of our aunts, uncles and cousins as well. I still have many photos taken on these trips and at the family gatherings from all those years ago.

"By the late 1950s, my younger brother and sister were also married, going on to start their own homes, and, sadly, Dad had passed away. Mum found that the family home had become too big for her and so she moved to a maisonette in Emmer Green where she enjoyed living for many years."

This page shows photos of those to whom this book is dedicated

Pearl's parents, Stan and Joan,
in the 1940s with Stan in his wartime Navy uniform.

Paul after his first day at Reading School in September 1979.
He is in the back garden of his grandparents, Stan and Joan.

Melvyn and his friend BJ on holiday in Devon in the late 1950s.

Melvyn on duty with the RAF Police at RAF Gan in the Maldives in the early 1960s.

Peggy in her Land Army uniform during the Second World War.

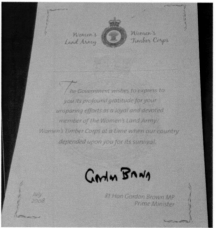

The medal and certificate awarded in 2008 to Peggy
for her service in the Land Army.

Patrick's Mum, Grace, sitting on the back of a motorbike
with her sister, Audrey, in front.
This photo was taken in the 1930s in Staverton Road outside their home.

The Coronation Street Party in 1953 taking place in Shirley Avenue. The man
in the dark suit on the left is Patrick's Dad. In the background can be seen the
pre-fab houses on the right and the semis at the back.

Pearl on her tricycle in her grandparents' back garden in Cressingham Road in the early 1950s.

Dennis with son Paul in Stan and Joan's back garden. This was taken shortly after Dennis, Pearl and Paul moved back to Whitley in 1969 – on the hill.

Young Patrick in the back garden of his home in Shirley Avenue in the late 1940s.

In the front garden of Peggy's childhood home in Linden Road are her children, Mary-Ann and Alan, together with Pearl and their young cousin, Neil, in the late 1950s

Miss King's class at George Palmer Junior School performing
the Nativity play in 1975

The Christ Church choir, taken after Sunday morning service
in the late 1970s.
The choirmaster and organist Leslie Davis is stood towards the right.

Patrick

Patrick's parents were married at Christ Church in 1938, his mother having lived with her parents until then in a house in Staverton Road which they had occupied since it was built in the early 1930s. They had both worked at Sigmund Pulsometer Pumps (SPP) in Oxford Road which was where they met. After their marriage, they moved into a new house in Shirley Avenue in Whitley Wood. Patrick had an older brother, Michael, who was born in 1939, just after the start of the Second World War. He himself was born at the house in 1947........

"Mum and Dad both worked at SPP and some of Mum's colleagues got together and decided that they would engineer a date for the two. Some of her friends told Mum that a young man called Wally seemed very interested in her and would like to meet her. Some of Dad's friends told him that Grace who worked in wages was keen to go on a date with him. So Dad sheepishly asked Mum for a date and they started going out together. They went out for several years and were married at Christ Church in April 1938 with Mum's two younger sisters, Margery and Audrey, as bridesmaids. The party duly set off from Staverton Road to make the journey to Christchurch.

"My brother was born in October 1939 and was a handsome young man always popular with his classmates at the newly opened Ashmead School, which he attended after leaving Ridgeway School. Most of the children at Ashmead were from the houses surrounding the school on Whitley Estate although some would have been from Shirley Avenue. Michael enjoyed school and, as Ashmead had a Junior School of Building, which covered the building trades and engineering, he learnt lots of practical skills as he was not particularly academic. Like my father he loved working with his hands and making things. He got an engineering apprenticeship and worked at Robert Cort in Elgar Road as an engineer. He was quite artistic and good at drawing and eventually became an engineering draughtsman.

"Just before the war Dad left SPP and got a job working for Miles Aircraft Limited at Woodley Aerodrome. At the outbreak of war Dad volunteered to join the army but, because of his job being a reserved occupation, he was rejected. He continued to work there until about 1946 when he was working on the new jet engines with Frank Whittle. Subsequently, the technology was given to the Americans and Dad opted to train as a supply teacher attending college at Chalfont St Peter in Buckinghamshire and going to Normandy in France to learn French. I do know that, at the time he went to Normandy, he had only 30 shillings (£1.50) in his bank account. He couldn't afford to buy a dressing gown and Mum had to make one from an old army blanket for him to take with him!

"When I was a child, the world was a much simpler and happier place or so it seemed to me. We were an average family and lived in a 1938 mid-terrace house. At the side of our right-hand neighbour's house was an eight-foot wide alleyway that ran round to the back of our four houses. It was only a cinder track so if you fell over it could be quite painful.

"We only had two bedrooms so my brother and I had to share a bedroom which was not ideal as there was eight years' difference between us. Again, apart from the kitchen, we had only one living room and so we had to get on with one another as it would have made it awkward not to. Dad was very practical and he made a cabinet for our record player from an old tea chest and then we had the television on the top. The kitchen had a crane boiler and in the winter it kept the room very warm especially if Mum put the fish and chip wrappers on it on a Friday. We did not have a washing machine but we did have a gas boiler and a hand mangle for doing the washing.

"In the back garden we had a small lawn and a large old fashioned rose tree as well as a coal bunker. Dad was keen on model engineering and made a model steam locomotive which he ran on a track in the back garden. He also had a large greenhouse where Mum grew her plants. Dad grew Nicotiana (Tobacco plants), which he dried out before rolling them up for cigarettes. My memories of Mum were her love of gardening and her green fingers. She loved growing chrysanthemums and hers were brilliant and she won many prizes at the South Reading Horticultural Society in Basingstoke Road. Mum was also quite artistic and won prizes for flower arranging as well.

"Shirley Avenue was in the shape of a letter J and Woodside Way formed the bar of the J across its top. In Woodside Way, which joins Whitley Wood Road, there were several large semi-detached houses on both sides before it reached Shirley Avenue, which had bungalows stretching as far as the bend in the road outside my home after which there were about seven prefabricated houses. Behind the last prefab, there was some open land and beyond that was a ditch. Beyond Woodside Way lay common land which extended as far as the boundary with RAF Shinfield Park. The Officers' houses were off of Whitley Wood Lane and there was a boundary hedge between them and the Rifle Ranges which were nearer the main part of the Park. Whitley Wood Lane used to go on to join Brooker's Hill in Shinfield but that road was later cut when the Motorway was built.

"The RAF used to have the most wonderful fireworks on bonfire night and, as children, it was a big treat to be allowed to go and see them setting off the bonfire and the expensive fireworks. Better still it was free and, as we did not get much pocket money, that was a bonus. My pocket money was about half a crown at that time (12.5p per week). That bought more than you might think at the new sweet shop cum barbers (Maynard's) that had just opened at the start of Northumberland Avenue. Liquorice sticks were 1d each (0.5p) and traffic lights (large gobstoppers that changed colour and made your cheeks ache if you had too many) were also 1d each but a packet of aniseed balls was 2d.

"Not many people had cars so we children tended to play in the alleyways (hide and seek, etc. was very popular). The fields at the far end of Shirley Avenue provided an area for us to make camps and the like or go scrumping apples from the apple trees behind the allotments, which were in Whitley Wood Lane, just after the entrance to the Cook's Estate. The apples were very bitter and may even have been crab apples so quite why we bothered to scrump them I am not sure but we did!

"Although we were lucky enough to have a 9" Bush black and white TV, you could only watch children's programmes until 6 pm then there was a watershed till 7.00pm when the adult programmes came on. There were no computers or the like so you could read a book or comic, watch TV when it was on or listen to the radio or go out playing in the street or the fields. We were expected to be back by 9:30 or 10:00 pm though. Quite often however we would play on the triangle of grass outside the four houses in our terrace. It was frowned upon for boys and girls to play together and I recall as a child arguing in favour of letting one of the girls who wanted to play in our game to be allowed. I actually persuaded my friends to let her join us which she did.

"Saturdays were the big days for a 3d bus ticket into town and a visit to the station, where you could buy a platform ticket for 2d (1p) and watch the steam engines shunting or the express come through to Bristol or Paddington. If you were really lucky you could be allowed on the footplate of a locomotive to see how they stoked the fire. I can recall watching the railwaymen with their shiny caps and feeling my cheeks getting hotter with the warmth of the fire coming at me. Strangely enough it always seemed to rain on a Saturday. When you got back it was time to have dinner and I always enjoyed my dinner.

"Sometimes on a Saturday we would walk to John Warwick & Sons timber merchants in Basingstoke Road and buy some offcuts of wood, which we had selected as being most useful from the pile of scrap from the sawmill. There were all sorts of wood and usually you could take an old pram to load it into. We would ask the man through the porthole how much it was and he had a blind box on the window cill. More often than not he would say "Oh just put a shilling in the blind box", so we would gather a shilling and put it in the blind box before pushing the loaded pram to the house of whoever had an old pram chassis and wheels. There we would construct a trolley which we could take turns to ride.

"Beyond the alley to our house lived another family and their little girl and they had a cocker spaniel called Baron who would bark at me every time I walked down the alleyway, except once when he escaped and bit my leg. I can recall walking along with Baron's teeth firmly embedded in my leg and me trying to get him off!

"Behind our row of houses were a hedge and then a large field, which was a pig farm that had an entrance in Whitley Wood Lane. Every Saturday night there was an awful squealing of the pigs which I assume was when the farmer killed them. We often used the field to make a shortcut to the next field where there was a large pond. That was where a small group of houses was later built by James T Cook, the local builders.

"One of my earliest memories was of a street party in 1953 for the coronation of Queen Elizabeth II. In those days no one stood on ceremony and there were no anti-monarchists or demonstrations, etc. I suspect that most people felt like having a celebration and the coronation of the new Queen seemed a suitable event. Everyone brought out their kitchen table and from the bend outside our house there must have been at least ten six foot long tables complete with crepe paper tablecloths. Children were dressed as different characters. I cannot remember what I was wearing but my friend Terry Mills was dressed as Simple Simon. Unfortunately, Terry spilt lemonade all down his outfit and was very upset about it. There was a lot of food as well including cakes, which were quite a luxury as sugar had only just come off ration. Everyone mixed together and it didn't matter who you were or whether you lived in a prefab, a terraced house or a bungalow as all the food and all the drinks were pooled. Generally there would have been Simmonds Brown and possibly sherry for the ladies or even gin but, at 10s. (50p) a bottle, gin was quite expensive. There may even have been some whisky as families seemed to have a bottle of whisky or brandy for medicinal purposes or if someone special came to visit. The mothers all did the cooking and serving and the children gorged themselves as I recall. It was all terribly politically incorrect but that was how Britain was in the 1950's. I think that the coronation party was the real highlight because each child was given a coronation mug as a keepsake.

"Terry Mills and I were good friends. He was the eldest son in the Mills family. His father was a Cockney and ran a painting and decorating business and they had a car. As I recall it was a Standard Flying 9 and I can remember riding in the back and waving to the people rather like the Queen does on state visits.

"As children, whatever happened, we knew better than to say to our parents that we were bored as we would be told to "find something to do". When the field where the Cook's houses were built was sold (now Falmouth Road) we realised that, as work progressed, we could use the site as a playground, which we did. We didn't do any damage and merely clambered over piles of bricks and up the scaffolding. In particular I remember an occasion when I was standing on the scaffold boards at the top of one house when the watchman came round with his dog. We all jumped into the pile of sand fifteen feet below us and ran like mad. Unfortunately for me I forgot to bend my knees when I jumped and I was in some pain but I still managed to outrun the watch and his dog.

"There was a large hedge between this development and the prefabs at the end of Shirley Avenue and we would break off willow branches and attach a piece of clay and flick it at each other over the hedge. Unfortunately for me one day someone decided to throw a brick over the hedge and it caught me on the head and I literally saw stars and there was quite a bit of blood coming from my head. Some friends managed to help me get back home, but not before a lady who happened to be passing asked me if I was alright. I replied that I thought I was and thanked her. When I got home, Mum bathed the wound and wrapped a towel round it to stem the flow of blood. One neighbour very kindly offered to take us to the Battle Hospital in Oxford Road and off we went. Mum was worried about not getting blood on the car seats but I was enjoying a ride in a brand new car so I suppose it was a fortuitous accident for me. I do not think I suffered any permanent damage from the injury but I can still see where the brick struck my head after all these years.

"I attended both the Infants and Juniors at Geoffrey Field School and I can recall that there was the Bourne Methodist Mission Hall just opposite where we sometimes took lessons until one of the pupils set light to the piano! I remember that when my Geoffrey Field School blazer became threadbare at the elbows Dad would stain the bare threads with green Dylo dye to conceal them. I can laugh at that now but I was horrified at the time; however most families where we lived were in the same position. I later went on to Ashmead School. In 1959, when I was 12, we moved around the corner to Whitley Wood Road. When I left Ashmead at the age of 15, I went to work for a local estate agent called Wright Brothers in the Harris Arcade at £3 per week and I enjoyed every minute of it."

Pearl

These memories are those of Pearl, my wife, who has lived in or near Whitley for most of her life......

"I was born in Battle Hospital and was taken home by my Mum and Dad to Cressingham Road, where they were living with my Nan and Grandad. I had a happy childhood living there. In better weather, I would ride my tricycle or play with my toys in the garden. I enjoyed pushing my doll's pram while walking along with my Mum when she was going shopping in Northumberland Avenue.

"My Grandad kept a lovely front garden with straight hedges on three sides and also kept colourful flower beds. When he was working in the garden, people passing by used to compliment him on them. He was often asked how he kept the hedges so straight and he answered that it was all done by eye.

"I used to go down with Grandad to the back garden shed where he had benches down the side, a stove in the middle and a wooden chair. On the bench he kept his garden tools, which were neatly laid out, and also three different-sized iron lasts, which were used for shoe repairs, together with a tin containing rubber soles and different-sized segs. There was a hole in one bench where he would put a last and then carry out the shoe repairs, when needed, finishing them off with a good polish.

"On one side of the path, Grandad grew vegetables at the bottom of the garden behind the shed. On the other side, Dad used to grow large-headed single chrysanthemums which he grew up sticks. He covered each bloom with a brown paper bag, which he tied loosely underneath with string to stop earwigs getting in the flower head. Mum and Nan wouldn't have appreciated earwigs being brought indoors in cut flowers!

"Mum used to take me to the garden gate to wait for Grandad to come home on the works bus from AWRE Aldermaston. The bus dropped him at the Whitley Library at the bottom of Cressingham Road. As soon as Mum saw him coming, I was allowed to run down the hill to meet him. I used to enjoy skipping up the road holding his hand.

"Dad worked at the University of Reading, based at the London Road campus, and travelled to and from there on his bike. In those days, a lot of people cycled to work because they worked locally. He enjoyed working there and continued until he retired after 39 years' service. "When I was 5, I went to Ridgeway Infants School. Mum took me there on a little seat at the back of her bike. On the way home we would sometimes stop at my Nan's in Linden Road as it was close to the school. I would tell Nan what I had been doing that day and Mum could have a chat with her.

"The pace of life was so much slower then. On a Sunday, there were no shops open except the newsagents for the Sunday papers. In the summer, you could see people cutting the grass and gardening. Some of the children went to Sunday School. Mums would be cooking the Sunday roast which most families had at midday. After lunch people might go to visit their families and would stay for tea. Others might go out for a walk. After tea, some families might go to The World Turned Upside Down where the parents would sit in the garden while the children played on the swings. This was a time to relax before the working week began and the children were back at school.

"I enjoyed going shopping in town with Mum and Nan as I used to get a ride on a double-decker bus, the No. 23, which started its journey from part way up Cressingham Road. On our return from town, we would get off at the corner of Staverton Road. As there was no roundabout, the driver had to reverse the bus from Cressingham Road into Staverton Road with the help of the conductor. The driver would then take it to the bus stop in Cressingham Road ready to go into town and, often, people would be waiting there.

"On a Saturday at teatime, Mr Peck would come round the streets with his horse and cart carrying fruit and vegetables which the local people would go out to buy. While he was serving his customers, the horse was kept occupied with a nosebag of hay to chew on. Sometimes in the winter, when Mum went out to buy vegetables from him, it was such thick fog that you could just about see the cart by the light of the lamps on it. He needed the lamps so that he could see when he was weighing out the goods on his big scales and taking the money. On occasion, the muffin man came round the street, carrying his tray of muffins on his head, holding the tray with one hand while the other hand was ringing his bell.

"The home in Cressingham Road was the hub of the family. There was quite often one of them popping in. As soon as someone came to see her, Nan would put the kettle on for a pot of tea and cut a slice of Dundee cake. On cold days there was a lovely coal fire in the grate. I used to enjoy Nan's hot buttered toast which she would cook on a toasting fork in front of the fire. Nan's teapot is still in the family to this day as it holds such special memories and it is being looked after by her grandson Barry.

"When I was nearly six, my Mum and Dad were able to move into their own home as there were new houses being built on the old Honey's Farm land, also known as Home Farm. The land was off Northumberland Avenue at the top end near the George Palmer Schools. Just before my sixth birthday, we moved into our new home backing onto Long Barn Lane park. It was lovely having the park at the bottom of the garden. Twice a week, the baker would call and bring a basket of bread and cakes from the back of his van to our front door for Mum to choose what she wanted to buy (she liked a crusty loaf and would sometimes choose cream buns or cream slices). Also, nearly everyone had their milk delivered to the doorstep every day by the Co-op or Job's Dairy milkman.

"As George Palmer Infants School was much nearer, I moved from Ridgeway School ready for the autumn term. When I was put into my first class, it was in a wooden hut, which had a big stove in the middle to keep it warm and had tables and chairs round the room for us to attend our lessons. The teacher's name was Miss Joy. I moved on to the George Palmer Junior School at the end of that school year.

"After we had been living in our new home for about a year, I remember Dad buying his first car and we used to love going down to Hayling Island for the day on a Sunday with a picnic, often taking my cousin, Carol. It was easy to travel there because there was hardly any traffic on the roads then. On other Sundays, we might go to Finchampstead Ridges for a walk in the afternoon, especially in the autumn when the trees were very colourful, and I took my dog, Snowy, who loved to run about among the fallen leaves.

"My Mum and Dad had known Betty and Alan, who lived next-door, since their school days. After they had settled in, they found that there were allotments available nearby so Dad and Alan each rented allotments to grow their own vegetables. I liked going with Dad to help him lift some of the vegetables he had grown. Later, they had to give them up as the land was to be developed, which was a shame as they had enjoyed their time spent there.

"My Aunt Lily used to take my friend Eileen and me for a walk down an unmade lane with big hedges either side, which I think was Manor Farm Road, so that we could pick wild flowers and blackberries. The roadside was covered with cow parsley. It was like being in the country. We would go back to her house for cake and a glass of lemonade then Uncle Tom took Eileen and me back home while taking their dog, Trixie, for a walk.

"When I was walking home from school with Marlene, a friend who lived along the road from me, we might have pennies to spend in a newsagents in Northumberland Avenue called Twitchett's, where we could buy an iced Jubbly or choose penny sweets, which were laid out on the counter, or we might choose some sherbet lemons or winter mixture from the big jars on the shelf. Miss Twitchett would weigh out on the scales the ones we chose and put them in a paper bag for us.

"After school, I would sometimes sit on the front doorstep with Carol, a friend who lived next door, and we might play five stones or swap beads. Other games we might play were two-ball up the wall, hopscotch, skipping or hula hoop. In those days, there were no computers or mobile phones so we were outside playing games until we were called for our tea.

"After tea, I went to the park and enjoyed playing with friends on the swings and roundabouts. Sometimes we used to sit on the grass, pick daisies and make daisy -chains. In those days there was a park-keeper, who had a little hut close to the entrance in Long Barn Lane. After I had gone home, I used to be able to hear him blow his whistle to warn everyone to leave when he was about to close the park in the evening by locking the gates.

"The local policeman, PC Tims, lived in Canterbury Road. He was often to be seen cycling around the area. When he was not working, he would leave his helmet in the middle of the sideboard in front of the window so people knew there was a policeman living there.

"After the Juniors, I went to Katesgrove Secondary School for a year until George Palmer Senior Girls had moved to Southlands School in 1960. Then the building was prepared for Katesgrove Senior Boys and Girls to move in as the new Cintra School. While at Cintra School, I used to go to Cintra Park to play hockey and tennis and to Arthur Hill's swimming baths for swimming lessons.

"When I left school, I started work at Milwards in Broad Street. As a teenager, working in a shoe shop in the 60s and seeing all the latest fashions, I was keen to buy the new styles as they came in. I always seemed to be saving up for the next new pair of shoes or boots! After a few years, I left Milwards to work at Sunley Building in Garrard Street, in the offices of GPO Telephones (later to be called BT).

"While at Milwards, I made some new friends. I often went out with them in the evening. We used to go to the Olympia ballroom for dancing and to see the top pop groups of the day, including The Hollies and Georgie Fame and the Blue Flames. It was a popular venue in the town for young people and was often very full. Also popular was the Alex in London Street where there would be a DJ on a Sunday evening playing hit records of the time. One record that sticks in my mind is 'Little Red Rooster' by the Rolling Stones.

"At the same time, Dennis was going to the Olympia with his friends and we got to know each other. After courting for a while, we got engaged and, a couple of years later, we were married at Christ Church, where Mum and Dad had also been married. We made our home in Northumberland Avenue at the top of the hill. Our son, Paul, went to George Palmer Infants and Junior Schools and then to Reading School which he thoroughly enjoyed. When he was about six, he went for swimming lessons in the Avenue School pool after his school day had finished. Having learnt to swim, he went on to gain his personal survival medals at Arthur Hill's swimming baths and then to train with Reading Swimming Club at the Central Pool. He started Sunday School at Christ Church when he was seven and then thought he would like to join the church choir. After being assessed by the choirmaster, Leslie Davis, he became a chorister. He went on to join the men's choir and to be a crucifer and server at Christ Church. The family has very happy memories of those times."

Pearl's Parents

Pearl recalls going with her Mum or on her own to her Nan's Cressingham Road home and spending time chatting about the family and the surrounding area. She is most grateful for that time because it has left her with many precious memories of what life was like for her Mum and Dad (Joan and Stan). These are some of their memories told by Pearl.....

"My Nan and Grandad had moved into Cressingham Road when it was first built in the 1930s. Their children, Tom, Joan and Ken, were then very small. They had moved from Awbrey Terrace off Orts Road in Newtown. My Mum had gone to Newtown Infants School at four where she remembered being taught to knit, which she enjoyed and she became very accomplished at it.

"After they had moved when she was six, Mum went to George Palmer Infants and Juniors and then on to the Palmer Central School at 11. [As my son, Paul, and I went through the George Palmer Infants and Juniors as well, there were three generations of the family who had attended the schools at various times over the years. When I went to Cintra School, Dad recalled that my school's headmaster, Mr Tuggey, had also taught him as a boy at Redlands School].

"Mum remembered walking down Northumberland Avenue towards Whitley Wood with her friends in the 1930s, picking blackberries from the hedgerows. The area was not built up and there were fields of the local farms all the way down to the cottage with the lighthouse, which particularly stuck out in her memory.

"Dad told the story that he used to help the milkman deliver milk before going to school. He would ride on the cart and then take the milk from the cart to put on the doorstep of the house where they were delivering. He said that, on a Sunday morning, he would go to St Barnabas Church and, during the singing of hymns, he would sit with the organist and pump air into the bellows to make the organ work. He used to say that, by the end of the service, it had made his arm ache!

"Mum recalled joining the Girl Guides with her friend, Vera, at Tyndale Baptist Church at the top of Cressingham Road. They both enjoyed going to Guides and went camping with them over the weekend. Mum remembered having their meal round the camp fire and then all having a good sing-song.

"After leaving school, Mum went to work at the offices of Greenslades, the printers, in King's Road. Not long after she started work, the Second World War began. Mum used to tell with pride how first her older brother, Tom, joined the RAF and then later her younger brother, Ken, joined the Royal Marines and how smart they both looked in their uniforms. She also said that, in the Great War, Grandad had been in the Navy, having joined as a regular sailor in 1912. Meanwhile, Nan was working at Hill's in Broad Street, who sold prams, pram accessories and baby clothes, and one of the jobs she used to do was to fine-stitch the trim around pram hoods. Nan and Grandad were married in 1919, a year after the Great War ended.

"During the Second War, Mum went dancing at St Giles Hall and it was there that she met my Dad who was in the Navy. She told me that he used to walk her home from the dance when he was on leave but, when he was away at sea, Mum used to walk home in the black-out from St Giles Hall with her girlfriends. They had to pass the air raid shelters (one Anderson shelter being in the footpath down the road from her home in Cressingham Road) but she said that they didn't ever feel at all afraid!

"While Dad was away at sea, Mum said that she used to walk up to see my Nan and Grandad in Linden Road. She used to go into the garden with Grandad and he would pull her some carrots, which would be washed ready to take with her. She recalled enjoying eating one as she walked down Cressingham Road on her way home. The year after the War ended, Mum and Dad were married at Christ Church and, after their honeymoon, they lived with my Nan and Grandad in Cressingham Road. I was born a couple of years later and Mum used to say how much she enjoyed taking me out in my pram and walking into town to do her shopping.

"Sometimes, on a Wednesday afternoon, Mum would take me to see my Nan at Linden Road. They would have a chat and a cup of tea. While there, my Aunt Roma, who worked at Huntley and Palmers biscuit factory, would sometimes give us a bag of broken biscuits, which could be bought there and were very popular with the staff.

"Mum knitted a lot of lovely cardigans for me when I was growing up. Later on, she knitted Arran jumpers for her young grandson, Paul. She was also good at needlework, making me some very pretty dresses when I was a child. Mum used my Nan's Jones sewing machine to make them. She bought some patterns which involved smocking on the front of the dress. However, when I was older, Mum told me that she hadn't found smocking work easy to do. One day, Dad had offered to have a go at it and, to her surprise and delight, he had made an excellent job of it. When Mum showed it to Nan, she could not believe that he could achieve such delicate work having never done it before! Many more dresses were made with Dad doing the smocking work.

"After we had moved from Cressingham Road into our own home, where houses had been built on the Home Farm land, Mum and Dad would often say that they liked living there, particularly as there was a large grass island at the front and the garden backed on to the park. It remained the family home for the next 60 years."

SOURCES AND REFERENCES

A Dictionary of Biographies of Architects in Reading, Sidney Gold

Victoria County History of Berkshire, ed. W Page and PH Ditchfield, 1923

The Road To Worton Grange: Simonds' and Courage's Brewery at Reading 1785-1980, T A B Corley, 1980

A Draught of Contentment, John Pudney, 1971

The Growth of Reading, Malcolm Petyt, 1993

Reading Transport 1901-1976, 75 years of municipal transport, Reading Transport, 1976

George Palmer Central School Reading 1912-1952, ed. GA Winterton, Headmaster, 1952

Official Opening of Southlands Secondary School for Girls 22 November 1960, Proceedings, 1960

Parish of St Giles-In-Reading, Leslie Harman, 1946

History of Education in Reading, Leslie Harman, 1960

The Story of Reading, Daphne Phillips, 1990

The Story of the Town of Reading, W M Childs, 1905

The Top of Whitley, Daphne Barnes-Phillips, 2002

So many hearts make a school, Daphne Barnes-Phillips, 2007

Victorian Architecture in Reading, H Godwin Arnold, 1976

Bricks and Mortals, Reading Girls' School, 1994

History of Christianity in Reading, Leslie Harman, 1952

Reminiscences of Reading, An Octogenarian, 1888

An Ecclesiastical History of Reading, P H Ditchfield, 1883

History of Ridgeway Primary School (1929-2002), Mary Wheway, 2002

Northcourt Avenue – its history and people, Penny Kemp, 1996

Leighton Park – The First 100 Years, Various, 1989

Abstracts from the Vachell Papers, 17th Century, held in Reading Central Library.

The Avenue School. Records taken from the log books of the School and from staff.

The Church Bells of Berkshire, Frederick Sharpe, 1970.

Domesday Book – Berkshire, ed. John Morris, 1979.

Various street directories, census records, press cuttings, at Reading Central Library.

INDEX

Scallop Shell Press

Who we are

Ever since the Middle Ages the scallop shell has been the symbol of those going on pilgrimage to the shrine of St James in Compostela, Spain.

Today pilgrimage is even more popular than ever as people of all faiths, and none, seek a meaning for their journey through life.

The shell became a metaphor for the journey, the grooves representing the many ways of arriving at one's destination. At a practical level the shell was also useful for scooping up water to drink or food to eat.

Scallop Shell Press aims to publish works which, like the grooves of the shell, will offer the modern pilgrim stories of our shared humanity and help readers arrive at their own meaningful interpretations of life.

We hope that our books will be shells within whose covers readers will find an intellectual and spiritual source of sustenance for their own personal pilgrimages.

John and Lindsay Mullaney

Some other published titles

Reformation, Revolution and Rebirth, John Mullaney and Lindsay Mullaney

Reading's Abbey Quarter. An Illustrated History, John Mullaney

The Reading Abbey Stone. John Mullaney

François Longuet and the Reading Mission, Lindsay Mullaney

The Timms Family of Reading and London, Katie Amos

Early Closing Day, Mike Cooper

If you would like to find out more about Scallop Shell Press please visit our website

www.scallopshellpress.co.uk